WITHDRAWN

THE GREAT EDUCATORS

Rousseau

AND EDUCATION
ACCORDING TO NATURE

Thomas Davidson, M.A., LL.D.

CHARLES SCRIBNER'S SONS
New York
1898

Republished, 1970
Scholarly Press, 22929 Industrial Drive East
St. Clair Shores, Michigan 48080

Copyright, 1898, By
CHARLES SCRIBNER'S SONS

Library of Congress Catalog Card Number: 70-108469
Standard Book Number: 403-00427-6

LB
518
D3
1970

This edition is printed on a high-quality,
acid-free paper that meets specification
requirements for fine book paper referred
to as "300-year" paper

PREFACE

In my volume on ARISTOTLE in this series, I tried to give an account of ancient, classical, and social Education; in the present volume I have endeavored to set forth the nature of modern, romantic, and unsocial Education. This education originates with Rousseau.

With much reluctance I have been obliged to dwell, at considerable length, on the facts of his life, in order to show that his glittering structure rests, not upon any broad and firm foundation of well-generalized and well-sifted experience, but upon the private tastes and preferences of an exceptionally capricious and self-centred nature. His Émile is simply his selfish and unsocial self, forcibly withheld, by an external Providence, in the shape of an impossible tutor, from those aberrations which led that self into the "dark forest" of misery. If my estimate of Rousseau's value as an educator proves disappointing to those who believe in his doctrines, I can only say, in excuse, that I am more disappointed than they are.

In preparing the present volume, I have depended solely upon the original sources, the works of Rousseau himself, and these I have allowed to speak for themselves. I owe a certain amount of direction, and a few dates and references, to Mr. Morley's *Rousseau*.

THOMAS DAVIDSON.

"GLENMORE,"
KEENE, ESSEX CO., N.Y.,
January 31, 1898.

CONTENTS

CHAP.		PAGE
	INTRODUCTORY	1
I.	IDEAS AND ASPIRATIONS CURRENT IN ROUSSEAU'S TIME. — AUTHORITY, NATURE, AND CULTURE	3

ROUSSEAU'S LIFE

II.	FORMATIVE PERIOD	24
III.	PRODUCTIVE PERIOD	50
IV.	ROUSSEAU'S SOCIAL THEORIES	77

ROUSSEAU'S EDUCATIONAL THEORIES

V.	INFANCY	97
VI.	CHILDHOOD	113
VII.	BOYHOOD	137
VIII.	ADOLESCENCE	156
IX.	YOUTH	178
X.	MANHOOD	203
XI.	CONCLUSION. — ROUSSEAU'S INFLUENCE	211
	BRIEF BIBLIOGRAPHY	245
	INDEX	247

ROUSSEAU

INTRODUCTORY

The Educational System of Rousseau forms an integral part of a complete theory, or philosophy, of human life, individual, domestic, social, economic, political, and religious. This theory, again, is compounded of elements mainly derived from two sources, (1) a somewhat incoherent body of ideas and aspirations current in Rousseau's time and in the centuries immediately preceding him, and (2) his own character, as formed by native endowment, education, and experience. The latter source makes a very large contribution; for among all writers of influence there is hardly one whose personality, that is, whose feelings, emotions, and tastes, enter for so much into his writings, as Rousseau's. He is, above all, subjective, and, indeed, the apostle of subjectivism. This is what he stands for in history.

In order, then, to understand the pedagogics of Rousseau, we must begin by making as clear as possible to ourselves that body of ideas and aspirations which gave form and direction to his thought, and then consider his experience and character, as furnishing the matter of the same. Having done this, we shall be in a position to account for his theory of human life, and to see how his system of education is conditioned by it. We shall then find little difficulty in expounding that system itself, or in distinguishing what is objective and, therefore, permanent in it, from that which, being due to transitory notions or personal tastes, is subjective and temporary. Finally, and with this distinction in our minds, we shall be able to trace the effect of Rousseau's thought, as a whole, upon subsequent theory and practice, and to show how his educational teachings have influenced later systems, for good or for evil, down to the present day.

CHAPTER I

IDEAS AND ASPIRATIONS CURRENT IN ROUSSEAU'S TIME

AUTHORITY, NATURE, AND CULTURE

> Questo modo di retro par che uccida
> Pur lo vinco d' amor che fa natura.
> * * * * *
> Per l' altro modo quell' amor s' obblia
> Che fa natura e quel ch' è poi aggiunto,
> Di che la fede spezial si cria.
>   DANTE, *Inferno*, XI., 55, 56, 61-63.

IF true human greatness consists in deep insight, strong and well-distributed affection, and free, beneficent will, Rousseau was not in any sense a great man. His insight, like his knowledge, was limited and superficial; his affections were capricious and undisciplined; and his will was ungenerous and selfish. His importance in literature and history is due to the fact that he summed up in his character, expressed in his writings, and exemplified in his experience, a group of tendencies and aspirations which had for some time been half blindly stirring in the bosom of society, and which in him attained to complete consciousness and manifestation for the first time.[1]

---

[1] Rousseau has been undeservedly blamed for feeling and expressing this. In the opening of his *Confessions* he says: "I feel my heart, and I know men. I am not made like any that I have seen,

These tendencies and aspirations, which may be comprehended under the one term individualism, or, more strictly, subjective individualism, have a history, and this we must now sketch, if we are to understand the significance of our author.

Modern individualism is a reaction against the extreme socialism of the Middle Age. The ruling principle of that age was authority, conceived as derived from a Supreme Being of infinite power, and vested in the heads of two institutions, Church and Empire, or, more frequently, in that of the Church alone.[1] According to the views then prevalent, the individual was neither his own origin nor his own end. He was created by God, for God's glory,[2] and was merely a means to that. He had therefore, of course, no freedom, whether of thought, affection, or will. Free inquiry into the laws and nature of reality gave way to a timid discussion of the meaning of authority. The natural affections were but grudgingly admitted to a place in life, and, even as late as the Council of Trent, in the sixteenth century, an anathema was pronounced upon any one who should say that the state of vir-

---

and I venture to think that I am not made like any that exist. If I am not better, I am, at least, different. Whether nature did well or ill in breaking the mould in which she cast me, no one can tell till after he has read me." The truth is, Rousseau was the first of a new type, of which there are plenty of specimens in our day, the type of the subjective, sensuous, sentimental, dalliant, querulous individualist. Nature by no means broke the mould. See Morley, *Rousseau*, Vol. II., pp. 304 sqq.

[1] See Dante, *De Monarchia*, and compare Bryce, *The Holy Roman Empire, passim*.

[2] "In His will is our peace," says a blessed spirit in the *Paradise* of Dante (III., 85).

ginity and celibacy was not better than the state of matrimony.¹ Above all, free self-determination of the will, possible only through free inquiry and free affection, was placed under the ban. The task of the centuries since the close of the Middle Age has been gradually to shake off this yoke and to restore men to freedom, that is, to convince them that they are ends in and through themselves.

The first notable manifestations² of this tendency were the Germanic Reformation and the Italian Renaissance, both belonging to the sixteenth century. The former claimed freedom for the individual intelligence; the latter, freedom for the individual feelings and emotions. Neither of them thought of aspiring to freedom of the moral will, which is the only true freedom. This is a fact of the utmost importance in enabling us to comprehend the thought and practice of the sixteenth, seventeenth, and eighteenth centuries. We look vainly in these for the conception of moral freedom.³ What the absence of this meant, we can perhaps most clearly see, when we realize that the complete, logical outcome of the Reformation was Voltaire; that of the Renaissance, Rousseau. It takes the clear, mathematical mind of the French to carry principles to their logical conclusions in thought and

---

¹ See Denzinger, *Enchiridion Symbolorum et Definitionum*, p. 231, § 856.

² We can trace the tendency itself back to Abélard (1079–1142), and even further.

³ In Gœthe's great drama, Faust, who stands for the complete movement toward individualism, and who discovers its nature and limitations, takes his stand upon the will. "*Allein ich will!*" he says, in defiance of all Mephistopheles' suggestions. Part I., l. 1432 (Schröer).

practice.[1] What Rousseau demands is absolutely free play for the feelings and emotions. But it took a long time for any one to become clearly aware that this was the true meaning of the Renaissance.

In trying to escape from authority, the men of the Reformation appealed to Reason; those of the Renaissance, to Nature. And the causes of this are obvious. Reason can find justification only in Reason; feeling, emotion, as claiming to be guiding principles, must look for theirs in Nature. Accordingly, while among the "Reformers" Reason played the chief part, and in the end gave rise to speculative philosophy, among the "Humanists" Nature received a homage which finally developed into physical science. The notion of "Nature" was an inheritance from the Greeks, chiefly, it should seem, through Plato. Indeed, the distinction between Nature ($\phi\acute{v}\sigma\iota\varsigma$) and convention ($\theta\acute{\epsilon}\sigma\iota\varsigma$), or law ($\nu\acute{o}\mu o\varsigma$), is fundamental in Greek thinking, which may be said to have originated in an attempt to find in Nature, regarded as unerring because necessitated, a sure refuge from the manifold forms of capricious-seeming conventions.[2] Already in the minds of the Greeks this distinction involves that dualism between the material and the spiritual which pervades almost their entire philosophy, and constitutes its chief defect. Accepting, without analysis, the ordinary, common-sense view of the world, which regards material things as entirely indepen-

---

[1] See Mrs. Browning, *Aurora Leigh*, Bk. VI.

[2] See, especially, Plato's *Cratylus* and the opening lines of Æschylus' *Agamemnon*. Cf. Lersch, *Sprachphilosophie der Alten*, Vol. I., pp. 1 sqq.

dent of thought, and governed by laws more rigid and reliable than it can claim, they were fain, like many equally unschooled scientists of the present day, to adopt these laws as the norm for human action; in a word, to naturalize spirit. Continuing to think, however, they were finally surprised to discover that Nature itself was purely conventional ($\theta\acute{\epsilon}\sigma\epsilon\iota$, $\nu\acute{o}\mu\varphi$), that is, subject to the laws of spirit, and therefore incapable of furnishing a court of appeal from these. This was the work of the Sophists, who, by their open scepticism, made it very clear that, if there was any inexorable law, it must be sought elsewhere than in Nature. Socrates wisely sought it in the unity and completeness of thought; but his work was undone by his pupil Plato, who sought it in a world of ideas of his own invention, a world having no necessary connection with either matter or mind. From this time on, Nature, and gradually mind or Reason also, fell into disrepute, and the supreme object of interest became Plato's fantastic creation, the so-called ideal world. This tendency, along with many other things in Greek philosophy,[1] passed over into Christianity, and reached its culmination in the Middle Age, when Nature and Reason were both equally regarded with suspicion, or even contempt,[2] as the origin of evil, and the place of Plato's ideal world was taken by an authoritative Revelation.

As we have seen, the Reformation undertook to rehabilitate Reason, and the Renaissance, Nature.

---

[1] See Hatch, *Hibbert Lectures* (1888), generally.
[2] See the horrified speech of the Archbishop, in *Faust*, Pt. II., Act i., lines 285-304 (Schröer).

They did so without attempting to overcome their opposition, or, generally speaking, to reject Revelation, at least openly. Thus it came to pass that the thinkers of the seventeenth century found, in their inheritance from the past, three unreconciled conceptions, or groups of conceptions, whose opposing claims they were in no position to settle [1] — Nature, Reason, Revelation. As might have been expected, some declared for one, some for another. Generally speaking, churchmen and their friends clung to Revelation and authority; while other thinkers tried to make peace between Reason and Nature. In general, the English mind showed a preference for Nature, and tried to explain Reason through it, while the French mind, setting out with Reason, could find no way of arriving at Nature, and so left the dualism unsolved. Bacon, Hobbes, and Locke form a strong contrast to Pascal, Descartes, and Malebranche. Rousseau generally follows the former, and especially Hobbes.

Hobbes conceived the human race as setting out on its career in a "state of Nature," which to him meant a state of universal war, resulting in a life "solitary, poor, brutish, nasty, and short." [2] At the same time he regarded Nature as "the art whereby God hath made and governs the world," getting over the paradox herein involved by maintaining that Nature "is by the art of man . . . imitated that it can make an artificial animal," [3] in other words, that 'art' is

---

[1] Most of the thought of the Western world, for the last three hundred years, has been devoted to effecting this settlement, thus far with very indifferent success.

[2] *Leviathan*, Cap. XIII. [3] *Ibid.*, Introduction.

an extension of Nature.[1] "Nature," according to Hobbes, "has made men so equal in faculties of the body and mind, as that though there be found one man sometimes manifestly stronger in body, or of quicker mind, than another, yet when all is reckoned together, the difference between man and man is not so considerable as that one man can thereupon claim to himself any benefit to which another may not pretend as well as he." And not only are men equal, but they have equal rights. "The right of Nature," he says, "which writers commonly call *jus naturale*, is the liberty each man hath to use his own power, as well as himself, for the preservation of his own nature; that is to say, of his own life; and consequently of doing anything, which in his own judgment and reason he shall conceive to be the aptest means thereto. By 'liberty' is understood, according to the proper signification of the word, the absence of external impediments." . . . "A 'law of Nature,' *lex naturalis*, is a precept or general rule, found out by reason, by which a man is forbidden to do that which is destructive of his life, or taketh away the means of preserving the same; and to omit that by which he thinketh it may best be preserved." In this "condition of war of every one against every one, . . . every one is governed by his own reason" and

---

[1] Shakespeare, *Winter's Tale*, Act IV., sc. iii.:

> "Yet nature is made better by no mean,
> But nature makes that mean: so over that art,
> Which, you say, adds to nature, is an art
> That nature makes. . . .
>   . . . This is an art
> Which does mend nature — change it rather: but
> The art itself is nature."

"every man has a right to everything, even to another's body. And, therefore, as long as the natural right of every man to everything endureth, there can be no security to any man." . . . "And consequently it is a precept, or general rule of reason, that every man ought to endeavor peace as far as he has hope of obtaining it; and when he cannot obtain it that he may seek, and use, all helps and advantages of war. The first branch of which rule containeth the first, the fundamental law of Nature, which is, to seek peace and follow it. The second, the sum of the right of Nature; which is, by all means we can, to defend ourselves. From this fundamental law of Nature, by which men are commanded to endeavor peace, is derived this second law: that a man be willing, when others are so too, as far-forth as, for peace, and defence of himself, he shall think it necessary, to lay down this right to all things; and be contented with so much liberty against other men as he would allow other men against himself." . . . "The mutual transferring of right, is that which men call 'contract.'"[1]

"From the law of Nature, by which we are obliged to transfer to another such rights as, being retained, hinder the peace of mankind, there followeth a third, which is this, that men perform their covenants made." . . . "In this law of Nature consisteth the fountain and original of 'justice.'" . . . "When a covenant is made, then to break it is 'unjust'; and the definition of 'injustice' is no other than the non-performance of covenant. And whatsoever is not

[1] *Leviathan*, Cap. XIV.

IDEAS AND ASPIRATIONS

unjust is 'just.'"[1] . . . "The agreement . . . of men is by covenant only, which is artificial; and therefore it is no wonder if there be somewhat else required, besides covenant, to make their agreement constant and lasting; which is a common power, to keep them in awe, and to direct their actions to a common benefit."[2] . . . "The only way to erect such a common power . . . is to confer all their power and strength upon one man, or upon one assembly of men, that may reduce all their wills, by plurality of voices, unto one will; which is as much as to say, to appoint one man, or assembly of men, to bear their person;[3] and every one to own, and to acknowledge, himself to be author of whatsoever he that so beareth their person shall act, or cause to be acted, in those things which concern the common peace and safety; and therein to submit their wills, every one to his will, and their judgments to his judgment. This is more than consent or concord; it is a real unity of them all, in one and the same person made by covenant of every man with every man."[4] . . . "He that carrieth this person is called 'sovereign,' and said to have 'sovereign power'; and every one besides his 'subject.'" . . . "The attaining of this sovereign power is by two ways. One is by natural force." . . . "The other is, when men agree amongst themselves to submit to some man, or assembly of men, voluntarily, on confidence to be protected by him against

---

[1] *Leviathan*, Cap. XV.

[2] Cf. Dante, *De Monarchia*, Bk. III., Cap. XVI.

[3] Used here in the sense of the Latin *persona*, for which see *Institutes* of Justinian.

[4] Cf. the story of Menenius Agrippa, Livy, Bk. II., Cap. 32.

all others. The latter may be called a political commonwealth, or commonwealth by 'institution'; and the former a commonwealth by 'acquisition.'"[1] . . .
" A 'commonwealth' is said to be 'instituted,' when a multitude of men do agree, and covenant, every one with every one, that to whatsoever man, or assembly of men, shall be given by the major part, the 'right' to 'present' the person of all of them, that is to say, to be their 'representative,' every one, as well he that voted for it, as he that voted against it, shall 'authorize' all the actions and judgments of that man, or assembly of men, in the same manner as if they were his own, to the end, to live peaceably among themselves, and be protected against other men. From this institution of a commonwealth are derived all the 'rights' and 'faculties' of him, or them, to whom sovereign power is conferred by the consent of the people assembled."[2]

Hobbes now goes on to say that the compact, thus once made, can never be either replaced or annulled; that it is binding on all; that the sovereign, once elected, can do no injustice, and hence cannot be put to death, or otherwise punished, by his subjects; that he has the right to prescribe or proscribe opinion, to determine the laws of property, to decide all controversies, to make war and peace, to choose all officials, to reward "with riches or honor," and to punish, "with corporal or pecuniary punishment, or with ignominy, every subject," and to confer titles of honor.[3] Though, theoretically speaking, the sovereign may be

[1] *Leviathan*, Cap. XVII.
[2] *Leviathan*, Cap. XVIII.
[3] *Leviathan*, Cap. XVII.

either a monarch, an aristocracy, or a democracy, yet Hobbes, for various reasons assigned, advocates the first. But, in any case, as soon as the sovereign is in power, "the liberty of a subject lieth . . . only in those things which, in regulating their actions, the sovereign hath pretermitted." This is the less to be regretted, that "liberty or freedom signifieth, properly, the absence of opposition; by opposition I mean external impediments, and may be applied no less to irrational and inanimate creatures than to rational."[1] Indeed, "liberty and necessity are consistent, as the water that hath not only liberty but a necessity of descending by the channel; so likewise in the actions that men voluntarily do; which, because they proceed from their will, proceed from liberty; and yet, because every act of man's will, and every desire and inclination, proceedeth from some cause, and that from another cause, in a continual chain, whose first link is in the hand of God, the first of causes proceed from necessity." . . . "And did not His will assure the necessity of man's will . . . the liberty of men would be a contradiction and impediment to the omnipotence and liberty of God."[2]

Hobbes' views with regard to law are characteristic. "The law of Nature," he says, "and the civil law contain each other. For the laws of Nature, which consist in equity, justice, gratitude, and other moral virtues on these depending in the condition of mere nature . . . are not properly laws, but qualities that dispose men to peace and obedience. When a com-

[1] This confusion of ideas was inherited by Rousseau.
[2] *Leviathan*, Cap. XXI.

monwealth is once settled, they are actually laws, and not before." . . . "The law of Nature therefore is a part of the civil law." . . . "Reciprocally, also, the civil law is a part of the dictates of Nature. For justice, that is to say, performance of covenant, and giving to every one his own, is a dictate of the law of Nature." . . . "Civil and natural law are not different kinds, but different parts of law, whereof one part, being written, is called civil, the other, unwritten, natural."[1]

We have made these long quotations from Hobbes, because he may be regarded as the father of that system of ideas which found their complete expression in Rousseau. Looking back on them, let us consider (1) what he borrowed from previous thought, (2) what he altered or added, and (3) what he arrived at. (1) He borrowed from Greek thought the notions of Nature ($\phi\acute{v}\sigma\iota\varsigma$) and convention ($\theta\acute{\epsilon}\sigma\iota\varsigma$), or law ($\nu\acute{o}\mu o\varsigma$), of necessity and freedom, and of hypostatic unity; from Latin thought, the notions of person and natural law;[2] from mediæval theology the notions of God's omnipotence and man's consequent dependence and unfreedom; and from "the judicious Hooker," apparently, the notion of a "social contract."[3] (2) He identified convention with nature, by making the former a mere conscious, that is, rational, expression of the latter;[4] and freedom with necessity, by calling

---

[1] *Leviathan*, Cap. XXVI. Note the naturalization of spirit!
[2] See Justinian, *Institutes*.
[3] See *Ecclesiastical Polity*, Bk. I.
[4] Here we have the germ of Hegel's objective and subjective reason, and, indeed, of modern idealism generally.

that which proceeds from a necessitated will, voluntary and, *therefore,* free. He assumed that men lived originally in a state of Nature, which was at once a state of freedom and a state of universal warfare, and that they passed out of that into a civic condition by a social contract, resulting in the creation of a new hypostatic person, of which all individuals thenceforth became mere organs. This new person, he maintained, had no real liberty of its own, but, being a product of Nature, was a mere implement in the hands of God, for His own ends. Thus (3), in his attempt to correlate Revelation, Nature, and Reason, or Convention, Hobbes arrived at the notion of a state or commonwealth as a mere automaton, whose motive force was externally communicated through its head — a notion which underlies many forms of theistic religion, for example, Islam and Calvinism, and finds its most complete realization in the Turkish and Russian empires of to-day. It is due to a mere shuffling and combining of old, unanalyzed concepts, such as those above enumerated, in a mind essentially servile.

But, though Hobbes was the avowed champion of moral determinism and political despotism, he unwittingly paved the way for freedom, by admitting that all sovereign or despotic rights were derived from a primitive convention. His readers forgot that this convention was, at bottom, due to Nature and God, and fixed their attention upon men as the source of civic rights. So true was this that even Charles II., Hobbes' pupil, was highly offended at what seemed a denial of the "divine right of kings." To maintain this right, Sir Robert Filmer wrote his *Patriarcha*,[1] which tried to show that all sovereign rights were derived from the sovereignty of the world originally conceded by God to Adam, and had descended in a direct line from him; hence, that all primitive equality among men and all occasion for a social contract were impossible. Princes are born princes; the rest of mankind, subjects or thralls. Against this plea for royal absolutism and popular enslavement, Locke raised his voice, and published in 1689, just after the revolution which expelled James II., his *Two Treatises on Government*. In the former of these he refuted, with needless gravity, the flimsy arguments of Filmer, and, in the latter, undertook to show what were the true origins of civil government.

Defining political power as "a right of making laws, with penalties of death, and consequently all less penalties for the regulating and preserving of property, and of employing the force of the community in the execution of such laws, and in the defence of the commonwealth from foreign injury, and all this only for the public good,"[2] he proceeded to consider how such power could rise. In dealing with this question, he made the two fundamental assumptions of Hooker and Hobbes, (1) that mankind started on its career in a state of Nature, in which all individuals enjoyed complete liberty and equality, (2) that the transition from this to the civic state was through a social contract; but he sided with Hooker, against

---

[1] *Leviathan* was published in 1651; *Patriarcha* was written before 1653, but not published till 1680.

[2] Bk. II., Cap. I., *ad fin.*

Hobbes, in maintaining that the state of Nature was not a state of war, but one of peace, governed by a natural law. "The state of Nature," he says, "has a law of Nature to govern it, which obliges every one, and reason, *which is that law*, teaches all mankind who will but consult it, that being all equal and independent no one ought to harm another in his life, health, liberty, or possessions; for men being all the workmanship of one omnipotent and infinitely wise Maker, all the servants of one sovereign Master, sent into the world by His order and about His business, they are His property whose workmanship they are, made to last during His, not one another's pleasure." Here we have to observe two things: (1) that, as in Hobbes, Reason is identified with the law of Nature, (2) that man is still conceived as being a mere instrument in the hands of a Higher Power. At the same time, Locke does not, on that account, deprive him of either moral[1] or political liberty, or submit him irrevocably to the tender mercies of a despot. He says: "To this strange doctrine, viz., That in the state of Nature, every one has the executive power of the law of Nature, I doubt not but it will be objected that it is unreasonable for men to be judges in their own cases . . . and that therefore God hath certainly appointed government to restrain the partiality and violence of men. I easily grant that civil government is the proper remedy for the inconveniences of the state of Nature, which must certainly be great when men may be judges in their own cases." . . . "But I desire those who make this objection to remember

[1] See *Two Treatises*, Bk. II., Cap. VI., § 58.

that absolute monarchs are but men; and, if government is to be the remedy of those evils which necessarily follow from men being judges in their own cases, and the state of Nature is therefore not to be endured, I desire to know what kind of government that is, and how much better it is than the state of Nature, where one man commanding a multitude has the liberty to be judge in his own case, and may do to all his subjects whatever he pleases without the least question or control of those who execute his pleasure? and in whatsoever he doth, whether led by reason, mistake, or passion, must be submitted to? which men in the state of Nature are not bound to do to one another." [1]

Locke not only rejects Hobbes' theory of despotic sovereignty, but he stoutly maintains that men, by submitting to common laws, do not lose, but gain, freedom. He says: "However it may be mistaken, the end of law is not to abolish or restrain, but to preserve and enlarge freedom." . . . "Where there is no law there is no freedom." . . . "For who could be free, when every other man's humor might domineer over him." [2] He holds that all property is rightfully due to labor, and all inequality of possession (wrongfully) to the introduction of money. [3] The origin of civil society is thus described: "Whenever any number of men so unite into one society as to quit every one his executive power of the law of Nature, and to resign it to the public, there and there only is a political or civil society. And this is done

---

[1] *Two Treatises*, Bk. II., Cap. II., § 13. Cf. Cap. VII., § 90.
[2] *Two Treatises*, Bk. II., Cap. VI., § 57.   [3] *Ibid.*, Cap. V.

IDEAS AND ASPIRATIONS

wherever any number of men, in the state of Nature, enter into society to make one people, one body politic, under one supreme government; or else when he joins himself to, and incorporates with, any government already made."[1] And Locke agrees with Aristotle in holding that men unite in this way because "man is by nature a political animal." "God," he says, "having made man such a creature that, in His own judgment, it was not good for him to be alone, put him under strong obligations of necessity, convenience, and inclination, to drive him into society, as well as fitted him with understanding and language to continue and enjoy it."[2] And Locke firmly believed, not only that all civil societies were due to original contracts, voluntarily entered into, but also that they might be dissolved when that contract was broken. Distinguishing, moreover, between society and government, which latter he held to be the act of a society already formed, he maintained that, when a government, or form of government, failed to perform the functions for which it was instituted, society might overthrow it, and put another in its place — an excuse for the revolution of 1688, and for revolutions generally.

Comparing Locke with Hobbes, we find a considerable advance, on the part of the former, in the direction of liberty. Men are no longer moral automata; they are no longer drawn into a social contract by mere selfishness, but by a beneficent law of their nature; the social contract no longer extends to the whole of human life, and is no longer irrevocable; by

[1] *Two Treatises,* Bk. II., Cap. VII., § 89.   [2] *Ibid.,* § 77.

such contract men gain, and do not lose, freedom, otherwise the contract is not binding; divine authority, though still freely acknowledged, does not prevent men from being the originators, and the only lawful originators, of their own governments; Reason is the qualification for free citizenship. Nevertheless, Hobbes' fundamental fallacies — the state of Nature and the social contract — still remain. The two Englishmen, Hobbes and Locke, were the chief inspirers of Rousseau's social and political theories. Of earlier men whose views tended away from mediævalism, such as Marsiglio of Padua (fourteenth century), Hooker (1553–1600), Machiavelli (1469–1527), Bodin (1530–1596), Grotius (1583–1645), Althusen, he knew very little, though he mentions some of them. Among his more immediate predecessors, the men that most influenced him were Montesquieu (1689–1755) and Morelly. The former, in his *Esprit des Lois*, first published at Geneva, in 1748, had dealt with social and political questions in an historic and scientific way, inquiring into facts, instead of spinning theories out of his own head or heart. Against this method, Rousseau, who hated research, and could not endure continuous study, but followed his "heart" in everything, protested with all his might, so that many of his theories may be said to come from a reaction against those of Montesquieu. Morelly, on the other hand, whose *Code de la Nature, ou le véritable Esprit des Loix, de tout tems négligé ou méconnu*, appeared in 1754, soon after Rousseau's second discourse (see Cap. IV.), and several years before the *Social Contract*, must have found in Rousseau a strong sympathizer. Though he combated Rousseau's notion that human corruption is due to the arts and sciences, and agreed with Hobbes, Locke, and Montesquieu in holding that man is improved by social culture, he was at one with Rousseau in maintaining that men in a state of Nature are good, and not bad, that most governments hitherto have rather corrupted them than otherwise, and that they have done this by permitting private property, and consequent inequality of possession, which is the source of all other inequalities and most other evils. He, accordingly, recommended a return to the simplicity and equality of Nature, by the establishment of a community of goods, that is, of socialism.

At the time when Rousseau began to write, the ideas of Hobbes, Locke, Montesquieu, and Morelly, and the questions started by them, were in the air. The chief of these notions were: (1) a state of Nature, as man's original condition, — a state conceived sometimes as one of goodness, peace, freedom, equality, and happiness, sometimes as one of badness, war, slavery, inequality, and misery; (2) a law of Nature, independent of all human enactment, and yet binding upon all men; (3) a social contract, voluntarily and consciously made, as the basis of justification for civil society and authority, — a contract by which men united for the protection of rights, and the enforcement of laws which had existed already in the state of Nature; (4) false inequality among men, as due to private property, or the usurpation by some of what, by natural right, belonged to all; (5) a peaceful, untroubled, unenterprising, unstruggling existence as the normal form of human life. The questions started were chiefly these: (1) Was the state of Nature one of freedom and peace, or of war and slavery? (2) Are Nature's laws beneficent or the opposite? (3) Do men gain or lose freedom through the social contract? (4) Are they improved or degraded by social union and culture? (5) Since all men are free and equal in the state of Nature, how do social subordination of one man to another, and social inequality come about, and what is their justification? (6) Are men bound to submit to social regulations against their wills?

In all these notions and questions there are two facts specially deserving of attention: (1) the ever-increasing importance assigned to Nature, and the ever-growing tendency to identify the divine will with its laws, and to regard Reason as the expression of these; (2) the growing tendency to look upon man as the originator of laws and the founder of institutions; as, therefore, their master and not their slave. It thus appears that, in the attempt to reconcile the three concepts of Revelation, Nature, and Reason, regarded as guides to human action, the first place came gradually to be assigned to the second, and all appeals to be made to it. And this fact was fraught with the gravest consequences, two of which may be here mentioned. (1) There was the gradual decline of theology and metaphysical speculation, with the growth of natural science. (2) There was the tendency to regard human duty as a mere docile following of Nature, and no longer as a process of abnegation of the natural self in favor of a loftier ideal.

In Nature, which thus became the watchword of the

time, men sought a quiet refuge from the warring subtleties of a theology and a philosophy which had lost contact with life, and left it devoid of interest. And though, for a time, they misunderstood Nature, and committed many enormities in their devotion to her, yet it proved in the end that "Nature never did betray the heart that loved her." Whatever view we may take of Revelation and Reason, it is certain that it is through the study of Nature, taken in its widest sense, that the truth of them becomes significant and fruitful for us.

It was while these ideas were fermenting in men's minds that Rousseau came upon the scene.

CHAPTER II

ROUSSEAU'S LIFE

(1) Formative Period (1712-1741)

Who would command must in command find bliss.
* * * * * * *
... Enjoyment vulgarizes.
    Goethe, *Faust*, Pt. II., Act IV., lines 5640, 5647.

HUMAN beings may, roughly speaking, be divided into two classes, — the dalliers and the willers, — into those who live for passive enjoyment, and those who live for active mastery. The former, endowed with keen sensibility and strong appetite (Plato's ἐπιθυμητικόν), which tend to direct attention upon themselves and upon immediate objects, and usually destitute of ambition, seek to enjoy each moment, as it passes, pursuing no definite path, but wandering up and down the field of time, like children, plucking the flowers of delight that successively attract them. As they are going nowhere in particular, they, of course, arrive nowhere. The latter, distinguished by courage and the spirit of enterprise (θυμός), which give their interests an outward direction, and by the stern quality of ambition, live mainly in the future, half ignoring the blandishments of the present, and finding their satisfaction in planning and carrying out great enterprises, which, when successful, give them position and fame — often a permanent place in the world's history.[1] Of the two chief literary inspirers of the French Revolution and of the individualistic tendencies of the present century, the one, Rousseau, belonged to the former class, the other, Voltaire, to the latter. How, then, it may be asked, did Rousseau come to be an important factor in a great historic movement? The answer is, For two reasons, (1) because, like other men of his type, he was thrown into circumstances which wounded his sensibility, and thus driven to imagine others in which it would find free play, and (2) because the movement in question was toward the very things which he represented, — sensibility, subjectivism, and dalliance. Over most of the men of his class, however, he had the rare advantage of being able to express his imaginings in literary form and in a style which, for simplicity, clearness, effectiveness, and almost every other excellence, looks almost in vain for an equal. Keen sensibility, uttered with confident and touching eloquence, is the receipt for making fanatics, and Rousseau made them. Meanwhile his ambitious rival, Voltaire, was making sceptics.

In treating of the life of Rousseau, it will be sufficient for the present purpose to consider only those events and experiences which, in a marked degree, contributed to form his character, and, through it, to make his writings what they are. Persons desirous

---

[1] Literary examples of the former class are Hamlet and Wilhelm Meister; of the latter, Julius Cæsar and Faust. In Mark Antony the characteristics of the two contend with fatal result. Cf. Tennyson's poem *Will*.

of knowing more will find ample details in his *Confessions*, perhaps the most recklessly impartial biography that ever was written, his *Rêveries*, letters, etc.

Jean-Jacques Rousseau, the second son[1] of Isaac Rousseau and of his wife Suzanne, *née* Bernard, was born at Geneva on the 28th of June, 1712. Both parents belonged to the *citoyen* class, the highest of the five classes into which the inhabitants of Geneva were divided; both were Protestants. The father, a watchmaker by trade, was descended from an old Parisian family, — his great-great-grandfather having emigrated from Paris and settled in Geneva in the early days of the Reformation (1529) — and retained all the characteristics of his French origin, — sensibility, liveliness, gallantry, romanticism, and love of pleasure. The mother, daughter of a clergyman, was a person of great beauty and refinement, but endowed with an almost morbid sensibility, which she had heightened by extensive reading of sentimental, highly colored romances, such as were current at the time. She died in giving birth to Jean-Jacques, who was thus left to the care of a father such as we have described.

It will be necessary to linger for a moment on the first years of our hero's life, because in them his character was formed to a degree that is very unusual. He was, in fact, a very precocious child, quick, vivacious, responsive, a very thunder-cloud stored with lightning feelings, ready to flash forth at any moment. At his birth he was taken charge of by an aunt, a sister of his mother's, a quiet, kindly person, much

---

[1] The elder son, seven years older than Jean-Jacques, ran away from home to Germany quite young, and was lost sight of.

given to embroidery and song-singing. She treated him with exemplary gentleness, not to say indulgence, allowing him to follow the bent of his own disposition, which, though free from any trace of malignity, continually drew him toward incontinence — to pilfering and devouring eatables — and to romancing; in plain terms, to lying. His sympathetic and winning nature, by saving him from correction, also prevented him from becoming aware of any moral principle, so that he passed his whole childhood without ever impinging upon any disagreeable *ought*, without any other guides than his own feelings. And this condition of things lasted during his entire life. He was always completely at the mercy of his feelings, acknowledging duty only for purposes of rhetoric.

As he was never allowed to go out and mix with other children in the street, he learnt very early to read and write; so that, by the time he was six years old, he was feeding his emotions and his vivid imagination upon the romances which had formed his mother's library. For over a year, his father and he used frequently to sit up whole nights together, reading aloud, in turn, the most sensational and sentimental stories, forgetting sleep in the nervous excitement and tearful rapture caused by pathetic love-scenes, heroic adventures, and hairbreadth escapes. Before he was seven years old (1719), his mother's library was exhausted, and then father and son were obliged to turn for nocturnal entertainment to the library of her father, which consisted of such works as Plutarch's *Lives*, Le Sueur's *History of Church and Empire*, Bossuet's *Lectures on Universal*

History, Nani's *History of Venice*, Ovid's *Metamorphoses*, and certain works of La Bruyère, Fontenelle, and Molière. Though not one of these seems to have been without its effect upon the child, that which most interested him was the first. Of this he says: "Through these interesting readings, and the conversations to which they gave occasion between my father and me, were formed that free, republican spirit, and that proud, indomitable character, impatient of yoke and of servitude, which have tormented me all my life, in the situations least suited for their manifestation. Continually occupied with Rome and with republican Athens, living, so to speak, with their great men, myself born a citizen of a republic, and son of a father whose strongest passion was his love of country, I was set aflame by his example; I thought myself a Greek or a Roman; I became the personage whose life I was reading; the stories of constancy and heroism which had struck me put lightning into my eyes and force into my voice. One day as I was telling at table the story of Scævola, the whole company was frightened to see me go up and hold my hand over a chafing-dish to represent his action."

Melodramatic romances and Plutarchic heroisms represented the world to the precocious, nervous, imaginative, secluded child, Jean-Jacques Rousseau, at the age of eight. The former rendered him dreamy and fantastic, the latter intractable and defiant. He himself says: "Thus began to grow and appear in me this heart at once so haughty and so tender, and this character, effeminate, yet indomitable, which, always hovering between weakness and courage, between dalliance and virtue, have all my life long placed me in contradiction with myself and caused me to miss both abstinence and enjoyment, pleasure and self-control." A sad and unpromising enough result of the first stage of education!

In 1720, when Jean-Jacques was eight years old, his father, in consequence of a dispute with an "insolent and cowardly" French captain, in which he felt himself unjustly treated, withdrew from Geneva, leaving his child to the care of a maternal uncle, who sent him, along with his own son, a child of the same age, to be educated in the house of a clergyman, named Lambercier, at Bossey, a village not far from the city. The cousins remained here for two years, and for the greater part of the time enjoyed themselves royally. The country, with all its beauty, freshness, and freedom, was new to them, and they rioted in it. They formed an ardent friendship for each other, and were inseparable night and day. They did not learn much — "Latin and all the trifling rubbish that goes with it under the name of education"; but they were, in the main, kindly and even indulgently treated, so that, while they were fond of their master, as well as of his sister, who acted the part of mother to them, they had but slight occasion to seek any other guide than their own tastes and appetites, or to learn the meaning of duty. It is easy to understand how, with an experience like this, backed by that of his earlier childhood, Rousseau came to believe in, and passionately to maintain, the natural goodness of the human character. To an incident which occurred toward the end of his sojourn at Bossey, namely, his being cruelly punished for a slight offence, — which, moreover, he stoutly maintained to the end of his days that he did not commit, — may be traced the origin of another doctrine of his, namely, that what confuses, degrades, and blasts human nature is discipline, the restraining or curbing of the natural impulses. The effect of this incident may be described in his own words: "Here came to an end the serenity of my childish life. From that moment I ceased to enjoy pure happiness, and to-day I feel that the recollection of the charms of my childhood stops there. We remained some months longer at Bossey; but we were as we are told the first man was, when, though still in the earthly paradise, he was no longer able to enjoy it; it was apparently the same situation, but in reality it was another mode of being. Attachment, respect, intimacy, confidence no longer bound the pupils to their guides; we no longer regarded them as gods who could read our hearts; we were less ashamed to do evil and more afraid of being accused; we began to hide, to mutiny, to lie. All the vices of our years corrupted our innocence and disfigured our games. The very country lost in our eyes that charm of sweetness and simplicity which touches the heart; it looked deserted and gloomy to us; it had covered itself with a veil, which hid its beauties from us. We no longer cultivated our little gardens, our herbs, our flowers. We no longer went to scratch the earth lightly, and shout with joy at discovering the germ of the seed we had sown. We were disgusted with life; our guardians were disgusted with us. My uncle withdrew us, and we parted with Mr. and Miss

Lambercier feeling that we had had enough of each other, and with small regret."

It would surely be impossible to write a severer criticism than this upon the sentimental, undisciplined, unmoral education which Rousseau, up to this time, had received, and which he afterwards put forward as the type of true education. So frail is it that a single experience of what he conceives to be injustice dashes the whole to pieces, turns his world into a desert, and sinks him in every sort of vice of which his age is capable — including even that of lasciviousness, prematurely developed in his ebulliently emotional nature, long nourished on sentimental romances. It is sad that we must allude to this painful subject here; but, unless we do, we cannot give a correct or fair account either of the man or of his teachings. He himself tells us that there ran in his veins "blood burning with sensuality almost from his birth," and, though he professes to have remained pure in action till late in youth, this is contradicted by facts which he relates. The truth is, his imagination was corrupt from early childhood, and he was a victim not only of sensibility, but of the demon sensuality, all the days of his life. Though this fact may move our pity, its effect upon his writings must not be ignored.

After leaving Bossey, at the age of ten, Rousseau remained, for a couple of years, along with his cousin, in the house of his uncle at Geneva. Here the two boys, mixing with no other children, attending no school, and having no definite tasks, made life a perpetual holiday devoted to amusement. They made kites, cages, drums, houses, bows, watches, marionettes. For the last they composed comedies, which later on they exchanged for sermons. Rousseau occasionally visited his father, who was settled at Nyon in the Pays de Vaud. Here he was petted and fêted by everybody, fell violently in love with several injudicious women of twice his age, sighed, wept, and went into hysterics over them, and was rewarded sometimes with candy. With all this, he remained a mere mass of impulses, ever tending to become more and more unruly, violent, and sensual, and without one ray of moral sense to guide them. So far, duty had played no part in his purely animal existence; so far, he had received no preparation for a human life. And such a life, a life involving regular habits, constant application, obedience, and self-denial, he was now about to be called on to lead. In a word, he had to learn a profession.

At first, when hardly twelve years old, he was placed in a notary's office; but found his occupation there so tiresome and unendurable that, though he did not show any signs of active rebellion, he was dismissed for ignorance and incapacity. He was then, in a crestfallen condition, apprenticed to an engraver, "a coarse, violent man," by whom he was treated as negligent and unruly apprentices usually were. "In a short time," says Rousseau, "he succeeded in tarnishing all the brightness of my childhood, in brutalizing my loving, vivacious character, and in reducing me, in spirit as well as in fortune, to the true condition of an apprentice." . . . "The **vilest tastes and the lowest rascality took the place** of my pleasant amusements, blotting them entirely from my mind. I must, despite a most sterling (*honnête*) education, have had a great tendency to degeneration; for this took place rapidly, and without the least difficulty." . . . "My master's tyranny finally . . . drove me to vices which otherwise I should have hated, such as lying, idleness, and theft." Comment on this is unnecessary, especially when we find Rousseau taking credit to himself for having but once stolen *money* — which he did at the age of forty! Lying he frequently pleads guilty to, not to speak of idleness. Yet he was not altogether idle at this time; for, in order to escape from the real world of work and duty, to which he neither then nor at any time knew how to adapt himself, he threw himself into the unreal world of romance, devouring, with the nervous excitement of his childish days, every thrilling or sentimental story he could beg or borrow.

His apprenticeship lasted about four years, and came to an end in a sudden and unexpected way. Having remained outside the city one night till after the gates were shut, and having been threatened by his master with severe chastisement for such offence, he resolved, rather than expose himself to this, to leave both his master and his home, and seek his fortune, as a knight-errant, in the wide world. His cousin, whose friendship had visibly cooled as Rousseau degenerated, made him a few presents, encouraged him in his resolution, and "left him without many tears." They never afterwards met or corresponded.

It was in 1728, when Rousseau was about sixteen

years old, that he resolved to become a "tramp," — for such, in very deed, he became. That he should do this need not surprise us. It was the logical outcome of his character and training, or, rather, want of training. It is training that fits us to be members of social institutions, and he had received no such thing, but had been left to follow his natural instincts, which were abnormally strong. Though he had been caged for a time, the only life he was prepared to lead was that of the wild bird, and to this he now, having made his escape, naturally enough betook himself. He was now to chirp and chatter, to fly hither and thither, as hunger and caprice might direct, to coo and make love and pilfer, utterly unaware that there is such a thing in the world as duty or self-denial. His master he blamed for everything. "Had I fallen into the hands of a better," he wrote, nearly forty years afterwards, "I should have passed, in the bosom of my religion, my country, my family, and my friends, a quiet, peaceable life, such as my nature demanded, amid regular work suited to my taste, and a society suited to my heart. I should have been a good Christian, a good citizen, a good husband and father, a good friend, a good workman, good in everything. I should have loved my calling, honored it perhaps; and, after having lived an obscure and simple, but quiet and even life, I should have died in peace in the bosom of my people. Soon forgotten, no doubt, I should have been regretted at least as long as I should have been remembered." The whole of Jean-Jacques is here. He would have been "good," as anybody can be, had he always found everything suited to his "taste" and "heart," that is, pleasant and attractive; but of heroic, moral goodness, in the midst of circumstances offending both taste and heart, he had not even a conception. Hence, when he found himself in such circumstances, he was bad, ready to shirk even the simplest and most sacred duties, and to descend to the utmost baseness.

It would be uncharitable to speak in this way of Rousseau, even though we but repeat his own statement, without good reason. But in the present instance such reason exists. His educational system has its chief source in his own experiences, tastes, and character, and cannot be appreciated in its moral bearings without an impartial presentation of these. By publishing his *Confessions*, moreover, he has invited us to make this presentation, which we can thus do without laying ourselves open to any charge of circulating malicious gossip or slander. In judging him as a man, we may allow him to put in the plea of King Lear, whom, indeed, he resembles in many ways: —

> "I am a man
> More sinn'd against than sinning."

After running away from his master, home, and relatives, Rousseau lingered for a short time in the neighborhood of Geneva, getting food and shelter as best he could, and rioting in the sense of animal liberty and romantic visions of a future career of pure, ebullient enjoyment suited to his "taste and heart." Here is one of them: "My moderation limited me to a narrow sphere, but one deliciously choice, in which I was sure to reign. A single castle bounded my ambition; favorite of the lord and lady, lover of the daughter, friend of the brother, and protector of the neighbors — that was enough; I asked no more." In the course of his rambles he passed over into Savoy, and at Confignon, finding himself penniless and hungry, he called upon the curé, a zealous Roman Catholic, who, by means of a good dinner and a bottle of wine, converted him to Catholicism. Rousseau always maintained that he received a most careful religious education; the above fact shows how much it meant to a sensuous nature destitute of moral discipline. To make sure of his proselyte, whose weaknesses he must have seen through, M. de Pontverre sent him, with a letter of introduction, to a recent convert, Madame de Warens, a person of many attractions and easy virtue, residing at Annecy. This lady, who lived on a pension from the King of Sardinia, received him kindly, fed and lodged him, and would gladly have given him a permanent home, which, as he fell in love with her at first sight, he would, no doubt, have accepted. But interested friends of hers succeeded in driving him away, and transporting him across the Alps to a monastery in Turin, there to undergo spiritual instruction and be formally received into the bosom of the Church. If, during his week's journey to Turin, he was in the seventh heaven of romantic ecstasy and hope, he found himself in quite another place on his arrival there. When the iron gate of the Hospice of the Catechumens closed behind him, he found himself in a gloomy prison, among men and women of the most degraded type, all paying with pretended conversion for a temporary subsistence. His account of his life there, and of his spiritual guides, beggars belief. His sojourn lasted but nine days,[1] at the end of which he solemnly abjured Protestantism, "received the accessories of baptism," and was admitted into the Church with gorgeous and edifying pomp. Then he was turned out into the street amid pious wishes, and with twenty francs of alms in his pocket. His romantic dreams had given place to a brutal reality.

Still he was not daunted. Finding food and lodging for a few cents a day, he idled as long as he could, scouring the city in all directions. When his purse was nearly empty, he tried to find work as an engraver, and, after many failures, managed to ingratiate himself with an attractive young shopkeeper, whose husband was at the time absent. He, of course, fell at once violently in love with her, and had hopes of reciprocation, when the husband returned, ordered him out of the house, and threatened him with a yardstick whenever he again came near it. A few days later, he found a place, as half-lackey, half-secretary, with a very worthy and gifted lady, whose only defect seems to have been that she kept him in his place and did not coquette with him. When, after a time, she died of cancer, he took the opportunity to steal a valuable ribbon, and when it was found in his possession, he said it had been given to him by a fellow-servant,[2] a young girl, it seems, of irreproachable

[1] Rousseau would have us believe that he was altogether three months in the hospice; but this, like many other things in the *Confessions*, is demonstrably incorrect.

[2] His reason for this, he says, was that, liking the girl and meaning to give her the ribbon, he had her in his mind!

character, and stuck to his lie, even in the presence of the girl, and notwithstanding her despairing appeals to him. He gained belief simply because no one was found bad-hearted enough to conceive any one capable of such cruel lying. Indeed, it seems hardly possible to descend to a lower depth of infamy than this, or to furnish a more drastic commentary on the sort of education which Rousseau received and advocated. And this is the man who is continually taking credit to himself for his chivalrous devotion to women, and speaking of them in the most effusive terms! The compunction which, in his *Confessions*, he so eloquently parades, only shows the value of rhetorical morality.

After leaving the house of Madame de Vercellis, Rousseau for a time prowled about the streets of Turin, often performing acts of so disgusting a nature that one wonders why he was not shut up in a madhouse. Once he was mobbed by an indignant crowd and escaped only by a barefaced lie. At the same time he was visiting a certain Abbé Gaime, who talked to him very seriously, gave him wise counsels, and made such an impression upon him as to be immortalized later in the *Vicaire Savoyard*.

At last a situation was found for him. The Comte de la Roque, a nephew of Madame de Vercellis, introduced him to the Comte de Gouvon, head of a noble family, who took him into his house as lackey, and promised to do better things for him. Here he was treated with great kindness, received instruction in Latin from the count's nephew, and for a while conducted himself satisfactorily, hoping, in course of time, to find his way into the good graces of the count's charming niece. Failing in this, and suddenly conceiving an ardent attachment for an old acquaintance of his apprenticeship days, he neglected his duties and his studies, was dismissed from his place, refused an offer to be taken back, and the two started off, with light-hearted glee, to resume the life of tramps. Rousseau recalled the delights of his journey to Turin. "What must it be," he thought, "when to the charm of independence is united that of travelling in company with a comrade of my own age, taste, and good humor, without formalities, *without duty*, without constraint, without any obligation to travel or to stop, except as we please. One would be a fool, indeed, to sacrifice such a chance for projects of ambition slow of realization, difficult, uncertain, and which, even if one day realized, were not, in all their glory, worth a quarter of an hour of true youthful pleasure and liberty."

The two young men had little money; but they hoped to make enough for board and lodging, by exhibiting a gimcrack, a Hiero's-fountain, in country taverns and bar-rooms. Disappointed in this, they nevertheless continued their tramp, with great jollity, across the Alps, arriving finally at Chambéry, ragged and almost shoeless. Here Rousseau, having made up his mind to return to Madame de Warens, with whom he had corresponded during his three years' stay in Turin, and not wishing to take his companion with him, began to treat him coolly, and the latter, taking the hint, embraced him, bade him good-bye, turned on his heel, and walked gayly off. The two never afterwards met. Their ardent friendship had lasted six weeks.

Madame de Warens, though surprised to see her *protégé*, whose fortune she had supposed made, come back to her in rags, nevertheless received him kindly, lodged him in her house, and, much to his chagrin, tried to prepare him for some sort of regular work. What he wanted was to dawdle about with her, to be caressed and petted, to follow the dear caprice of the moment, and to have no duties or definite employment. As Madame de Warens, at that time, hardly cared to be so completely absorbed, he was sent to a seminary to learn a little Latin, as a preparation for the priesthood. He hated his first teacher, but formed an ardent attachment for his second, who was weak and sentimental, but sympathetic.[1] In spite of this, Rousseau made little progress, and was soon dismissed for incapacity. He was thus thrown back on the hands of Madame de Warens, than which he desired nothing better. Music was next tried, with no better success, notwithstanding that he had great sensuous delight in it. He had not patience or persistence enough to learn even the rudiments of it, and was too vain to accept instruction from teachers. At last, Madame de Warens, getting tired, adopted a scheme to get rid of him. She sent him off to Lyons to accompany home a well-known musician of somewhat irregular habits, and during his absence went off to Paris without leaving any address behind. Rousseau deserted the musician in a fainting-fit in the

[1] Along with the Turinese M. Gaime, this man, M. Gâtier, went to form the portrait of the Savoyard Vicar. See p. 38.

streets of Lyons,¹ and hastened back to his dear
"mamma,"² as he called her.

Finding her gone, he "loafed" about Annecy for a
time, in somewhat disreputable company, and then
started off to convoy home to Freiburg Madame de
Warens' maid, whom, with his characteristic vanity
in such matters, he supposed to be deeply in love with
him. On the way he called, at Nyon, on his father,
who had married again, and had a satisfactorily affecting scene with him. Being, contrary to his expecta-
tion, coolly received by his companion's family, and
finding himself without money, he went to Lausanne,
persuaded a kindly innkeeper to board and lodge him
on credit,³ gave himself out as a Parisian, changed
his name, and set up as a music teacher. His almost
complete ignorance of music having soon been discovered, he, of course, made a ridiculous failure, and
soon left for Neuchâtel. On the way he had a fine
opportunity for Arcadian longings and self-pity. "I
must absolutely have an orchard on the banks of this
lake (Lake of Geneva), and of no other. I must have
a firm friend, a sweet wife, a cow, and a little boat.
Till I have all these, I shall never enjoy complete
happiness on earth." . . . "I sighed and cried like
a baby. How often, sitting down on a big stone to

---

¹ "He was abandoned by the only friend on whom he had a right
to count. I seized a moment when nobody was thinking of me,
turned the corner of the street, and disappeared." — *Confessions*,
Bk. I., Cap. III.

² *Maman.* She called him "Baby" (*Petit*). This was exactly
the relation that suited him. Cf. *Confessions*, Bk. I., Cap. II.

³ "I told him my little lies, as I had arranged them." — *Confessions*, Bk. IV.

weep at leisure, did I amuse myself by watching my
tears fall into the water!" At Neuchâtel he repeated
his experiment with somewhat better success than at
Lausanne; but, having one day fallen in with a Greek
archimandrite, who was collecting subscriptions to
restore the Holy Sepulchre at Jerusalem, he was glad
to follow him as interpreter, with the prospect of
much aimless wandering and good dinners. At
Soleure, however, the French minister, having satisfied himself that the archimandrite was a fraud,
sent him about his business, and took charge of Rousseau, who still pretended to be a Parisian. Having
heard the youth's story (Rousseau was now about
twenty), he gave him a hundred francs and sent him
off to Paris — home, as he thought! — to be attendant
to a young officer in the guards. During the fort-
night which Rousseau took to reach Paris on foot, he
had a royal time, filling himself full of visions of
future military glory, and then allowing them to
vanish in the more passive delights of idyllic landscape. Paris, of which he had heard so much, completely disappointed him, and, as his reception there
was not over cordial, he soon left it and trudged
southward, hoping somewhere to find his "mamma."
During this journey, he was once more in the seventh
heaven, although here and there he encountered experiences which tended to sober him, and which made
a lasting and fruitful impression upon him. Having
one day entered a peasant's house and asked for dinner, offering to pay, he received nothing but skimmed
milk and coarse barley bread, the man declaring that
he had nothing else. In course of time, however,

feeling that his guest would not betray him, the man opened a trap-door in the floor, descended, and returned with a ham, some good white bread, and a bottle of wine, on which, together with an omelette, Rousseau made a royal dinner. The peasant then explained to him that, in order to avoid ruin at the hands of the tax-gatherer, he was obliged to feign abject poverty. "All that he said to me on this subject," writes Rousseau, "was absolutely new to me, and made an impression that will never be wiped out. This was the germ of that inextinguishable hatred which grew up in my heart against the vexations endured by the unhappy people and against their oppressors."

Having, when he reached Lyons, sought out a friend of Madame de Warens', he learnt that she was at Chambéry, and would be glad to see him, having found for him a pleasant occupation that would not separate him from her. He hastened to find her; but, though offered a horse, he walked all the way. This was his last long journey on foot, the end of his vagabondage, which had lasted four years. He tells us that, though often poor afterwards, he never again had to go without a meal.

And here it is to be noted that this vagabondage had done five things for him: (1) It had satisfied his lust for adventure, and made him willing to settle down to a quiet life; (2) it had dispelled all the glamor attaching to courts, castles, palaces, and high life, and awakened in him a profound and enduring passion for rural simplicity; (3) it had made him acquainted, as hardly anything else could have done, with the character, lives, needs, and sufferings of the common people, and awakened in him a lively sympathy for them; (4) it had inspired him with a passionate love of natural scenery, such as no one before him had ever felt; so that he may fairly be called the inventor of the modern love of nature, the inspirer of the nature-poets of all lands; (5) it had made his language the expression of genuine passion and first-hand experience, and so given it a force which no style formed by reading or study ever can have. All these things told in the future.

For nine years, from 1732 to 1741, Rousseau spent the greater part of his time "at home," that is, with his "mamma." For four years they lived in Chambéry in a gloomy old house, under the most extraordinary conditions, and the most immoral, that it is well possible to conceive; for Madame de Warens had apparently no trace of moral sense. For two years Rousseau was employed in the public surveyor's office; but, as he found every sort of regular employment irksome and intolerable, he finally threw up his place and fell back upon his "mamma's" hands. After a season of blessed idleness, he once more took to teaching music, with a little better success this time. Most of his pupils were young ladies of good family, and he made a point of falling in love with nearly every one of them, as well as sometimes with their mothers and aunts. Observing this, and fearing for his morals, Madame de Warens ceased to treat him as a baby and admitted him to the closest intimacy. On the death of her other intimate, some time afterwards, Rousseau undertook to conduct her financial

affairs, which, on account of her recklessness and her
devotion to quacks and quackery, were rapidly falling
to irretrievable ruin. He only made them worse, taking
advantage of her recklessness like the rest. To
make matters worse, partly owing to certain accidents,
and partly to his own morbid imagination,
nursed on laziness, his health gave way and he became
an invalid for Madame de Warens to nurse. Being
fond of the country, he persuaded her to leave Chambéry
in the summer, and rent a cottage outside — the
famous *Charmettes*. Here he had everything his own
way, and for a time enjoyed perfect bliss. He had
his trees and flowers, his pigeons and bees, his mistress
and his books. His "languors" and "vapors"
gave him an excuse for avoiding all effort or trying to
earn anything, and so, for nearly a couple of years,
he dallied away his time, helping to devour the little
that remained of his poor mistress' pension, not to
speak of her patience. It is true that, to while away
the time, he did contrive to do a good deal of very
desultory reading, in all sorts of subjects, — geometry,
algebra, Latin, astronomy, and even philosophy. He
dabbled in Locke, Malebranche, Leibniz, Descartes,
and the Port Royal *Logic*. He even read some theology,
and was on the way to a wholesome fear of
hell, but was turned back by the comfortable optimism
of his mistress.[1] At last, both he and she desired a
change. He, having dabbled in physiology, came to

[1] It was a favorite idea of his that "the interesting and sensible conversations of a worthy woman are better suited to form the character of a young man than all the pedantic philosophy of books." — *Confessions*, Bk. I., Cap. IV.

think that his languors were due to polypus of the heart, and she encouraged him to go to Montpellier to be cured, starting him off in a sedan chair, as he was too feeble to ride! On the way, he fell into the most vulgar sort of intrigue with a coarse woman, and quite forgot his mamma — and his polypus. He, nevertheless, went to Montpellier and frittered away some months there. When his money was exhausted, he started off to join his new mistress; but, on coming to a point where the road to her parted from the road to his mamma, he virtuously chose the latter! His account of this deserves to be quoted: "As I approached Saint Esprit, I made up my mind to give Saint Andiol the go-by, and go straight on. I carried out this resolution courageously, with some sighs, I admit, but also with the inner satisfaction, *which I tasted for the first time in my life*, of being able to say: 'I deserve my own good opinion; I know how to prefer my duty to my pleasure.' This was the first real obligation I owed to study. This it was that had taught me to reflect and compare." . . . "One advantage of good actions is that they elevate the soul and dispose it to do better ones; for human weakness is such that one must count among good actions every abstinence from evil that one is tempted to commit. As soon as I had made up my mind, I became another man." We must not despise the day of small things!

It is well that virtue is its own reward; for in this case there was no other. On reaching the house of his "mamma," he was coolly received, and found that his place had been taken — taken by a travelling wig-maker of brusque, noisy ways. With a bleeding heart, he tells us, he voluntarily gave up his rights. "I kept this resolution with a firmness, I venture to say, worthy of the feeling which inspired it." . . . "The ardent desire to see her happy, at any price, absorbed all my affections." . . . "Thus began to spring up, with my misfortunes, those virtues of which the seeds lay in the depths of my soul, which study had cultivated, and which only awaited the influence (*ferment*) of adversity to bring them to fruition." In spite of his disappointment, Rousseau remained for some time with Madame de Warens; but at last, finding his position intolerable, went off to Lyons, to be tutor to the sons of M. de Mably, brother of the famous Condillac. In this capacity he was not a success, "having but three instruments, always useless, and often hurtful, with children,— sentiment, reasoning, anger." He seems, however, to have retained the good opinion of his employer, and he made several important acquaintances which were valuable to him in the future. His morals, too, improved somewhat; he stole nothing but wine. He kept his place for a year, and then, as usual, returned to his "mamma," who, though she treated him kindly, showed no desire to retain him. Nevertheless, he remained with her for some time; but, seeing that the renewal of the old relations was impossible, and that she was drifting to ruin, he at last left her, resolved to try his fortune in Paris, and hoping, — we may well believe sincerely, — if he were successful, to return and relieve her at a later time.

Here, in 1741, at the age of twenty-nine, Rousseau

passes, almost suddenly, from the dependent and passive period of his life to the independent and productive. Looking back upon the former, he says: "We have seen my peaceful youth glide by in a quiet, not ungentle sort of existence, without great troubles or great prosperities. This absence of extremes was, in large degree, due to my ardent but feeble temperament, slow to undertake and quick to be discouraged, shaking off inaction by fits and starts, but always returning to it from lassitude or taste; a temperament which, continually drawing me far away from great virtues and yet further from great vices, to the indolent, quiet life, for which I felt myself born, never permitted me to rise to anything great, in the way either of good or of evil." Though, after what we have seen, it is impossible to agree with the author in this indulgent estimate of himself, it nevertheless contains much truth. For the first thirty years of his life, Rousseau was a bundle of ardent desires, undisciplined by either serious reflection or moral training. He responded to outward impressions exactly as an animal does, restrained, if at all, only by fear. So utterly unaware was he that there is such a thing in the world as morality or duty, that it seems almost unfair to apply any moral standard to his actions. He is the natural man, pure and simple, with egoistic and altruistic instincts of a merely sensuous, not to say sensual, kind. He has gone back to the state of nature; he is a savage living among civilized men, and adapting himself to their standards as far as he must. He is lying, faithless, slanderous, thievish, lascivious, indecent, cruel, cowardly, selfish. Only toward the end do germs of nobler things begin to appear. Into what grotesque and portentous forms these developed, in the spongy soil of passion, and under the bitter rain of adversity, we shall see in the next chapter.

CHAPTER III

ROUSSEAU'S LIFE

(2) Productive Period (1741–1778)

I knew that all my talent came from a certain warmth of soul regarding the subjects I had to treat, and that it was only the love of the great, the true, and the good that could animate my genius. . . . I have never been able to write except from passion.

Rousseau, *Confessions*, Bk. X.

Rousseau's early education, failing to discipline his instincts, and leaving him in a state of animal spontaneity, had produced the man whom we have seen. Toward his thirtieth year, thanks partly to poor health, partly to rather extensive reading, he began, as we have seen, to realize his condition and to have dim glimpses, still in a sensuous way indeed, of a higher. His sated sensuality made him think of hell, while the vague thrill of delight which he felt in the presence of sublime nature was objectified into a god.[1] At all events, he began to make good resolutions, which is the first step in moral life. And he

---

[1] See *Confessions*, Pt. I., Bk. VI. It is perhaps worth noting that this is exactly the god of Faust, at the time when he is trying to ruin Gretchen. "Feeling is all," he says, at the close of a gush of immoral sentimentality. The result proves the moral value of such a god. Rousseau sat for much in the portrait of Faust.

was now about to enter a new school, very conducive to such life,—the school of experience, which, as Jean Paul says, is an excellent schoolmistress, though the fees are rather high.

In turning his face to Paris, Rousseau meant to win distinction and fortune as a musician. He had made considerable progress in musical knowledge and even aspired to be a composer. The idea of literary authorship had hardly yet dawned upon him. On his way he stopped at Lyons, where he obtained several letters of introduction, and had a momentary, but violent, love-spasm, which, however, did not detain him. "I reached Paris," he says, "in the autumn of 1741, with fifteen louis of ready money in my pocket, my comedy *Narcisse*, and my musical project as my sole resources. Having, therefore, no time to lose, I made haste to take advantage of my letters of introduction." He was well received. His "musical project," which was nothing less than a new system of musical notation, was presented to the Academy of Sciences, but failed to meet with the recognition he had expected. His *Narcisse*, though praised by Fontenelle and Diderot, with whom, among other notabilities, he had become intimate, was not then brought on the stage. He consequently relapsed, with a kind of desperate delight, into his habitual indolence, and would soon have been reduced to abject poverty, had not a wise Jesuit father advised him to try his fortune with the ladies. He did so, and, notwithstanding his incurable awkwardness and rusticity of manner, and his fatal habit of making effusive love to every woman he met, no matter what her rank or age, he was able, through one of his patronesses, Madame de Broglie, to obtain a situation as secretary to a recently appointed ambassador to Venice, the Comte de Montaigu. In this position, which brought him in contact with diplomatic and political life — in a word, with the "great world"— for the first time, he seems to have conducted himself with energy and firmness, though not always with prudence, and he retained it for eighteen months. He finally quarrelled with the ambassador, who was an incompetent, negligent coxcomb, and returned to France — without his salary. For a long time all his endeavors to obtain this were in vain — a fact which made a deep impression on him. "The injustice and uselessness," he says, "of my complaints left in my soul a germ of indignation against our stupid civil institutions, in which the true good of the public and real justice are always sacrificed to some indefinable, apparent order, in reality destructive of all order, and merely adding the sanction of public authority to the oppression of the weak and the iniquity of the strong." And this was not the only profound impression made on him by his sojourn in Venice. In his official life, he learnt the hollowness and corruption of diplomacy and officialism; in his private life, in which he saw much of the seamy side of Venice, he came to close quarters with forms of depravity that disgusted even his not over-healthy sensuality, and touched his better nature. He returned from "the most immoral of cities" a somewhat sobered and reflective man,[1]

[1] A letter which he wrote to a lady who received him badly on his return, because he had dared to quarrel with an ambassador,

and, what is more, with a little sense of his own personal dignity as a man.

On his return to Paris, Rousseau resumed his Bohemian life. For a short time he lived with a much-admired Spanish friend; but, on his departure, desiring to enjoy entire independence, he moved to a little inn near the Luxembourg, meaning to resume his musical studies and composition. His landlady was a woman of the coarsest sort, and most of the guests, Irish or Gascons, were like her, Rousseau being the only decent person among them! They were waited upon by a poor, hard-working girl, named Thérèse Le Vasseur, from Orleans, who soon became the butt of all the coarse ribaldry of the house. Rousseau alone took her part; a sympathy sprang up between them, which soon passed into what he called love, and in a few days the ex-secretary of the Venetian embassy, wishing to find a successor to his "mamma," as he says, made the poor creature his wife, in all but the name. He promised never to abandon her, and never to marry her, and he kept his word to his dying day, from 1744 to 1778. There is no accounting for tastes; and there is no doubt that Rousseau found in his Thérèse, who had

reveals his state of mind at this time. Here are some extracts: "I am sorry, madam; I have made a mistake. I thought you just: I ought to have remembered that you are noble. I ought to have felt that it is unbecoming in me, a plebeian, to make claims against a gentleman. Have I ancestors, titles? Is equity without parchment equity?" . . . "If he [the ambassador] has no dignity of soul, it is because his nobility enables him to be without it; if he is hand in glove with all that is filthiest in the most immoral of cities; if he is the chum of pickpockets; if he is one himself, it is because his ancestors had honor instead of him."

few personal charms, and who could never tell the time on a clock-face, remember the order of the months, or give change for a franc, what was permanently congenial to his sensuous, indolent nature. What he wanted was not stimulation or intellectual companionship, but steady, unexacting affection, and the thousand little soothing attentions that are quite compatible with gross stupidity. These he found, and his loyalty to her through all changes of fortune, amid good and evil repute, is perhaps the noblest trait in his whole life. What mattered it to him that other persons saw in her only coarseness and greed? he was content. "In the presence of those we love," he says, "feeling nourishes the intelligence, as well as the heart, and there is no need to go elsewhere in quest of ideas. I lived with my Thérèse as agreeably as with the finest genius in the world." . . . "I saw that she loved me sincerely, and this redoubled my tenderness. This intimacy took the place of everything for me. The future did not touch me, or touched me only as the present prolonged. I desired only to insure its duration. This attachment rendered all other sorts of dissipation superfluous and insipid. I went out only to visit Thérèse: her home became almost mine."

Rousseau's relation to Thérèse did one thing, at least, for him; it steadied him, and gave him peace to work. So he toiled away at musical composition, and tried, through his friends, to bring his work before the public, but without success. Discouraged at last, and having to provide, not only for himself, but also for Thérèse and her whole family, he attached himself, in a somewhat nondescript capacity, to certain wealthy patrons, who gave him a small salary. With these he passed the autumn of 1747 at the castle of Chenonceau, on the Cher, in great luxury; but, when he returned, a great surprise awaited him. His Thérèse was about to give birth to a child — an event for which he was not at all prepared. And here the worst side of his character, his utter want of any sense of moral responsibility and natural affection, came to the surface. As soon as the child was born, it was sent, despite the heartbroken remonstrances of the mother, to the foundling hospital, and was never again seen or recognized by its parents. We may anticipate somewhat, by adding that four other children, born to them later, all shared the same fate. With all his gushing sentimentality and sensuous sympathy, Rousseau recoiled from the tenderest, sweetest, and most sacred of all human duties, — the nurture and training of his own offspring. Speaking of the exposure of his second child, he says: "Not a bit more reflection on my part; not a bit more approval on the part of the mother. She groaned and obeyed." And this was the man who could not see her gibed by the Irish and Gascon abbés!

About this time, Rousseau became acquainted with Madame d'Épinay and Mademoiselle de Bellegarde, afterwards Comtesse d'Houdetot, both of whom were destined to play important parts in his life. Now also, mainly through his connection with the Abbé Condillac and Diderot, he began to think of literary composition, and planned a periodical to be called *Le Persifleur*, which, luckily, never saw the light. He did, however, write the article on Music for the *Encyclopédie*, which Diderot and D'Alembert were at that time preparing to issue. The progress of this work was interrupted by the arrest and imprisonment of the former, on account of his *Letter on the Blind*. Confined at first in the donjon at Vincennes, Diderot was afterwards, on his parole, allowed the liberty of the castle and park, and here his wife and friends visited him. Among the most enthusiastic of the latter was Rousseau, who went every other day. It was on one of these visits that an event occurred which affected his whole subsequent career, by throwing him into the path on which he gained both influence and fame. It must be described in his own words: "The summer of 1749 was one of excessive heat. It is two leagues from Paris to Vincennes. Unable to pay for a cab, I started at two o'clock in the afternoon and walked, when I was alone, and I walked quick to arrive the sooner." . . . "To moderate my pace, I resolved to carry some books with me. One day I took the *Mercure de France*, and, as I walked along reading it, my eye fell on this question, proposed by the Academy of Dijon as the subject of the following year's prize essay: *Has the Progress of the Arts and Sciences contributed to corrupt or to purify Morals?* On reading this, I instantly saw a new universe, and became a new man." . . . "If ever there was anything like a sudden inspiration, it was the movement that took place in me on that occasion. Instantly I felt my mind dazzled by a thousand lights. Crowds of brilliant ideas presented themselves all at once, with a force and a confusion which threw me into an inexpressible tumult. I became as dizzy as if I had been intoxicated. I was seized with a violent palpitation which made my bosom heave. No longer able to breathe while I walked, I threw myself down under one of the trees of the avenue, and there remained for half an hour in such a state of agitation that, when I got up, I observed that the whole front of my vest was wet with my tears, though I was not aware that I had shed any." . . . "If I could have written down a fourth part of what I felt and saw under that tree, with what clearness would I have exposed all the contradictions of our social system; with what force would I have laid bare all the abuses of our institutions; with what simplicity would I have proved that man is naturally good, and that it is solely through institutions that men become wicked!" . . . "On arriving at Vincennes, I was in a state of agitation bordering on delirium. Diderot perceived this. I told him the cause. He encouraged me to give vent to my ideas and compete for the prize. I did so, and from that moment I was lost. All the rest of my life and misfortunes were the inevitable result of this moment of bewilderment. My feelings rose, with utterly inconceivable rapidity, to the height of my ideas. All my petty passions were stifled by enthusiasm for truth, freedom, virtue; and what is yet more astonishing, this effervescence kept up in my heart for over four or five years, to a degree in which I have never known it to occur in the heart of any other man."[1]

[1] This translation is made partly from the *Confessions*, Pt. II., Bk. VIII., and partly from the second of the *Letters to M. Malesherbes*.

Such is Rousseau's account of his conversion to literature and to the advocacy of truth, right, and liberty. Though we need not accept its details as literal facts, we may fairly say that this conversion was due, not to calm conviction, based upon long and profound reflection, but simply to the direction of his ardent and effusive imagination upon a new and attractive series of Arcadian pictures of quiet bliss, contrasted with the noisy and distressing scenes in which he found himself. His essay won the Dijon Academy's prize, and this encouraged him to continue writing.

Meantime, he had hired a small apartment, furnished it, and taken Thérèse and her parents to live with him. Here he spent the next seven years, in a way which must be described in his own words: "The heart of my Thérèse was that of an angel. Our attachment increased with our intimacy, and we felt more and more every day how truly we were made for each other. If our pleasures could be described, they would excite a laugh by their simplicity: our private walks outside the city, where I munificently spent eight or ten cents at some alehouse; our little suppers by my window-sill, where we sat, face to face, on two chairs placed on a trunk which filled the embrasure. So placed, with the window as our table, we breathed the air, we could see the neighborhood and the passers-by, and, though on the fourth floor, look down into the street, while we ate. Who shall describe, who shall feel, the delights of those meals, consisting of nothing more than a quartern loaf of bread, a few cherries, a piece of cheese, and a half pint of wine, which we drank between us? Friendship, confidence, intimacy, sweetness of soul, how delicious your relishes are ! Sometimes we remained there till midnight, without being aware of it, or noting the time, until the old mamma called our attention to it." In this description we find the old vagabond Rousseau, only transferred to a city garret, and, at the same time, that ideal of a quiet, aimless, unenterprising, dalliant life, which underlies all his writings.

In Paris, Rousseau, notwithstanding his mode of life, and his ebullient, intractable disposition, made many friends both in the fashionable and in the literary worlds, and was recognized as a rising man, both in music and in literature. His opera, *Le Devin du Village*, was played, with great success, before the king at Versailles, and would have earned him a pension had he played his cards well. His *Narcisse* likewise was performed. His essay on the Moral Effect of the Arts and Sciences had identified him with certain rather paradoxical principles and made him an object of universal curiosity, so that he now resolved to live up to these even in externals. He gave up a public office which brought him a good salary, and took to earning his living by copying music. Another change must be described in his own words: "I began my reform with my dress. I left off gold facings and white stockings; I put on a round wig; I laid aside my sword; I sold my watch, saying to myself, with incredible delight, 'Thank heaven, I shall no longer need to know what the time is!'" In doing this, Rousseau wished to show that he, once for

all, identified himself with the common people, with
whom indeed his chief sympathies were. He was too
immediate and capricious ever to school himself into
the manners of polite society, or to find satisfaction
in its hollow formalities, and he would have been
wise had he avoided it altogether, as he did not. In
1753 he wrote his second 'discourse' — on the question, *What is the Origin of Inequality among Men, and
is it authorized by the Natural Law?* — which, though
failing to win the Dijon prize, added to his reputation,
and carried his thoughts further on in the direction
in which they had for some time been moving — that
of democracy.

In spite of all these successes, Rousseau got weary
of the close atmosphere of Paris, the obtrusive curiosity of visitors, and the calls of social life, — all the
more that he had for some time been suffering from
a painful malady. Accordingly, in 1754, he paid a
visit, in company with Thérèse, to his native city.
On his way he went to see his "mamma," whom he
found a poverty-stricken wreck. "Then," he says,
"was the moment to pay off my debts. I ought to
have left all and followed her, clinging to her till her
last hour, and sharing whatever might be her fate.
I did nothing. . . . I groaned over her and did not
follow her." At Geneva, he met with an enthusiastic
reception, returned, after twenty-six years of apostacy, to Protestantism, and was restored to his rights
as a citizen. He even made up his mind to settle
there for the rest of his life, and returned to Paris
with the intention of preparing for so doing. Finding, however, that Voltaire, whose unfriendly influ-

ence he dreaded, had settled near Geneva, and that the Introduction to his second discourse, in which he had spoken of the Genevese constitution, had given offence to his countrymen, he changed his mind, and, having just then received from his friend, Madame d'Épinay, the offer of a home in the charming Hermitage, near Montmorency, he accepted, and in the spring of 1756 removed thither, with Thérèse and her mother. The father, over eighty years of age, was packed off to the poorhouse, where he died almost immediately, to the great grief of Thérèse.

Amid the delights of his new residence, Rousseau was for a while in the most ecstatic condition. He had money enough to live on for some time, a fair prospect of paying work, devoted friends, self-set tasks in which he delighted, and natural surroundings in which he could thrill and gush to his heart's content. But this was too much. He did, indeed, continue to copy music; but his other tasks were soon mostly abandoned or forgotten, while he gave himself up to his natural indolence and dreaming. Withdrawing almost completely from society, he buried himself in the woods, and, with his morbid and lurid imagination, devoted himself to the creation of a Mohammedan paradise of sensual delights, in which he revelled day and night. From this time on, he never ceased to suffer from what may be called imaginative insanity. The effects of this showed themselves at the first touch with reality. Having been visited by the Comtesse d'Houdetot, the sister-in-law of his patroness, he at once enveloped her in all the products of his diseased imagination, and so conceived for her a frantic passion, whose depth he measured by the nervous derangement it caused in him, and the gush of passionate bombast it brought upon his lips.[1] Madame d'Houdetot, however, having not only a husband, but a lover besides, while allowing him to gush, did not respond as he desired, and the only result of his folly was that he embroiled himself with Madame d'Épinay, and many of his other friends. The former, a woman of very loose life, was jealous of her sister-in-law, while the latter, seeing the effect of solitude upon him, tried to induce him to return to Paris, or to separate from Thérèse, who, with her rapacious, deceitful mother, was bringing him to poverty, and becoming more and more a burden to him. For both women they undertook to provide. Rousseau, resenting all interference with his caprices, — they were nothing more, — suddenly left the Hermitage, and accused his friends of having formed a conspiracy, for which he could never assign any motive, to ruin him. One can excuse him only by saying that he was emotionally insane.

In the middle of December he moved with Thérèse to a rented cottage at Montmorency, having sent the mother about her business. Feeling himself here dependent on no one, and not being in very opulent circumstances, he began to work, and the next four years were the most productive of his whole life. They produced *The New Heloïse*, the *Social Contract*, and *Émile*. The first, which had been begun at the

---

[1] He maintained ever afterwards that she was the only **real love** of his life, that he had never completely loved even his "**mamma**," or his Thérèse at all ! Such is the power of a fixed idea !

Hermitage, under the influence of his passion for Madame d'Houdetot, was finished in 1759, and published two years later. The *Social Contract*, meant to be part of a larger work, *Political Institutions*, came out in 1762, only a few weeks before *Émile*.

At Montmorency, Rousseau made the acquaintance of the Duke of Luxembourg, Marshal of France, and his wife, who introduced him into their very aristocratic circle, made him acquainted with great people, and in every way treated him with the utmost kindness and consideration, so that in their society he had a season of comparative rest and comfort. He read the whole of *The New Heloïse* and *Émile* to the duchess in bed, and in consequence became a great favorite with her. She even undertook to see to the printing and publication of *Émile*, and made the contracts. Thus Rousseau began to feel that, after his stormy past, there might be in store for him a peaceful old age, with a competency, honor, and friends. But this was not to be.

No sooner had *Émile* appeared than it roused a storm, whose extent and fury it is, at first sight, difficult to understand. Within a month, the Parliament condemned the book, ordering it to be burnt and its obnoxious author arrested. To this result there is no doubt that persons who had once been his friends contributed. The truth is, Rousseau, by his book, had placed himself in opposition to two powerful and well-defined parties: (1) the orthodox, religious party, which included the court, (2) the philosophic or rationalistic party, at whose head stood Voltaire and the Encyclopædists — Diderot, D'Alembert, Grimm, etc. The latter was the prime mover in the storm. Voltaire and his followers had for many years been laboring, with might and main, to discredit and destroy all religion, all belief in the supernatural, and were flattering themselves that they would succeed in replacing it by what they called Reason. Now came Rousseau, whom they had in vain tried to add to their ranks, and not only reinstated religion and religious belief, but did so with a power and a brilliancy of literary style that threatened not only to defeat their purpose, but even to cast themselves and their works into the shade. This, of course, was not to be tamely borne. Voltaire especially, who hated Rousseau, and whose vanity shrank from no meanness, trickery, or deceit, moved heaven and earth to crush him; and he did this so adroitly that his victim was never able to trace to its source the persecution which remorselessly dogged him.[1] But if the party of Voltaire started the persecution, the orthodox party was but too ready to carry it on. The theology and religion expounded and advocated in *Émile*, especially in the Savoyard Vicar's *Confession of Faith*, not only set at open defiance all the dogmas of the Church, but were well calculated, by their simplicity and sweet sentimentality, to become widely popular, and undermine the Church's influence. Under these circumstances, we need not be surprised to find that the two mutually hostile parties combined to procure the condemnation of Rousseau and his book.

We have seen that the Duchess of Luxembourg had

[1] The infamous libel, which Rousseau so unjustly attributed to the Swiss pastor Vernes, was from the hand of Voltaire.

made the arrangements for the printing of *Émile*. It was through her he learnt that his arrest was about to be decreed. She had received a letter to that effect from the Prince de Conti, a friend of Rousseau's, and so great was her agitation, not only on account of the latter, but also on her own, that she roused him from sleep and called him to her bedside at two o'clock in the morning of June 9, 1762. It was intimated that, if he attempted to escape, no effort would be made to detain him. He accordingly determined upon this course, one chief motive being his unwillingness to compromise the duchess and her family. Several places of refuge were suggested to him; but he finally chose the nearest, Switzerland, and made all possible haste to reach it. On the way, he composed three cantos of a poem — *The Levite of Ephraim*. On reaching Yverdun, he stopped for a few days with a friend, considering what he should do next, where he should settle. He would gladly have gone to Geneva, but found it closed against him. There, too, his book had been burnt and a decree issued against him. "These two decrees," he says, "were the signal for a shriek of malediction against me from one end of Europe to the other — a shriek of unexampled fury. All the papers, journals, pamphlets, tolled the most awful tocsin." Despairing of finding a refuge in Switzerland, he turned to the canton of Neuchâtel, which at that time formed part of the dominions of Frederick the Great, and was governed by Marshal Keith, an exiled Scottish Jacobite of the noblest character. Though he had inveighed against Frederick, Rousseau, with his usual frankness, wrote to him,

telling him he was in his power and asking for an
asylum. The Prussian king not only granted him
this, but directed Marshal Keith to supply his needs,
and even build him a house, if he so desired. Rousseau declined his gifts, but thought better of him ever
afterwards. Marshal Keith proved to be the best
friend he ever had. Rousseau settled at Motiers, at
the foot of Mount Jura, and remained there for over
three years, having sent for Thérèse, his books and
papers. Though he frittered away his time in childish pursuits, writing almost nothing, things went well
enough till the departure of Marshal Keith, when the
people of the village, stirred up by narrow-minded
pastors, and prejudiced by the Armenian costume
which, on account of a troublesome malady, he had
adopted, began to threaten him with violence. This
finally went so far that he was obliged to leave the
place and betake himself to the Island of Saint Peter,
in the Lake of Bienne, in the territory of Berne.
Here he had reason to think that he would be unmolested, and, sending for Thérèse, gave himself up to
a life similar to that which he had for some time led
at the Charmettes, and later at the Hermitage. He
revelled in nature, botanized and sentimentalized from
morning till night, and was in an ecstasy of bliss.
His description of his life here is one of the most
charming Arcadian idyls in existence. At the end of
six weeks, however, his persecutors found him out,
and he received a peremptory order to leave the island,
and the territory of Berne, within twenty-four hours,
on pain of arrest and forcible expulsion. Stupefied
and almost heartbroken, he begged the authorities to

imprison him in the island for the rest of his life; he would then be safe, and he desired nothing better. But all in vain! He left the island in the end of October, 1765, not knowing whither to turn his steps. He thought of Corsica, of Berlin, where he would have had the protection of Marshal Keith, of England, which had been strongly recommended to him by certain of his patronesses, and where he hoped to enjoy the friendship of David Hume. He finally decided for the last of the three.[1]

The life of Rousseau from this point on, having no effect upon his chief works, may be sketched rapidly. We shall try to show merely how his undisciplined temperament, and the theories he based on it, led to their natural results. Some of these had already manifested themselves — a diseased, sensuous imagination, suspicion, willessness, querulousness, gloom. But others followed.

On his way to England, Rousseau went to Paris, to join Hume. Here, instead of being molested, he was lionized. "Voltaire and everybody are quite eclipsed by him," said Hume. In spite of this, Rousseau, who sincerely disliked publicity, was eager to proceed, and, early in January, 1766, he crossed over to England with his new friend. In London he received the utmost attention, was visited by the most distinguished persons, and was offered a pension by the king. About all this, however, he cared little, and was anxious only to find a quiet retreat. Several

[1] Rousseau's *Confessions* break off at this point. The projected third volume was never written. For what follows we have to depend on his *Rêveries*, correspondence, etc.

places were thought of; but he finally settled upon Wootton in Derbyshire. Here he was offered the use of a spacious house by a wealthy and generous Mr. Davenport, but insisted upon paying rent for it. Removing to it in March, and being soon joined by Thérèse, he resumed his life with Nature and his botany, set to work upon his *Confessions*, which he had long projected, and thought he was going to be happy. Soon, however, the rudeness of the climate, his ignorance of English, the difficulties caused by Thérèse, the change of feeling on the part of the English public, as evidenced by the press, and Hume's lack of continual satisfactory responsiveness to his ardent feelings, brought to the surface the morbid suspicion that lurked in his nature. He accused Hume of gross treachery, and of having conspired with Voltaire and D'Alembert to ruin him.[1]

Hume, it is needless to say, was guiltless of treachery; but his cold, passionless nature rendered him incapable of understanding the man he had undertaken to befriend, and with whose known infirmities he ought to have borne, while his vanity resented anything that seemed to call his Pharisaic impeccability in question. He accordingly printed a

[1] Among the charges which he brought against Hume was that of having written a letter pretending to come from Frederick the Great, which brought great ridicule upon him. The closing words of this letter, whose real author was the coxcomb, Horace Walpole, may be quoted, as containing some truth: "If you will persist in harrowing your soul to find new misfortunes, choose those which you prefer: I am a king and can procure you any sort you like; and I will do what you need not expect from your enemies, I will cease to persecute you when you cease taking pride in being persecuted."

defence of himself, thus dragging before the public what was essentially a private matter. The public took it up, and the world was deluged with pamphlets on both sides. Rousseau, who cared nothing for public opinion, preserved a dignified silence. Nevertheless, he became more and more unhappy, and, after sojourning a year at Wootton, he suddenly disappeared from it, leaving behind him Thérèse and his effects. He was found, first in Lincolnshire, and afterwards at Dover, whence, toward the end of May, 1767, he crossed over to Calais, a wretched man, full of fears, disordered in body and in mind.

For the next three years he wandered about from place to place, sometimes alone, sometimes the guest of generous patrons, among whom were the Marquis de Mirabeau and the Prince de Conti. In the château of the latter at Trye, near Gisors, he remained a whole year, under the assumed name of Renou, and here he wrote the second part of his *Confessions*. Having got into difficulties through Thérèse, whose character became daily more brutal, he suddenly left Trye, meaning to go to Chambéry and visit old scenes.[1] But he never reached that place. He passed some time at Grenoble, went thence to Bourgoin, where he spent over half a year, and informally married Thérèse, thinking thereby to regain her lost affection, and thence to Monquin, where he passed some fifteen months. Tired at last of wandering, and feeling that he might with safety return to Paris, he repaired

[1] His "mamma" was no longer living. She had died in destitution and wretchedness, in 1762, while he was at Motiers, botanizing and trifling.

thither in July, 1770, and settled down to his old
life, which he had abandoned fourteen years before,
when he went to occupy the Hermitage. Here he
passed eight years, living in a very simple way on a
meagre income, which he eked out by copying music.
He still continued, however, to botanize, to write,
and to compose music. His *Dialogues*, his *Rêveries*,
and some minor works belong to this period. He was
still visited by the great, the fashionable, the wise,
and the curious. But he was not happy. Thérèse
was daily becoming more trying; he suffered a good
deal of bodily pain; his mind was morbid, haunted
by phantoms from the past, fears for the present, and
gloomy forebodings for the future; he had lost many
of his friends, and his independence, which had almost
become a disease, forbade him to accept aid from
those whom he still retained. At last, however, by
the advice of his physician, he was induced to accept
the invitation of M. Girardin to go and live at his
estate of Ermenonville, some twenty miles from Paris.
He went there on the 21st of May, 1778, and was soon
followed by Thérèse. Country life seemed to bring
back some of his old enthusiasm, and he was revolving
in his head projects for the future, among them the
continuation of *Émile*, when, on the 2d of July, he
was suddenly taken ill, suffering acute pains. On
the following day he got up, and was preparing to go
out, when he was seized with violent shivering and
headache. While trying to swallow some medicine,
he fell forward on the ground, and almost instantly
expired, at the age of sixty-six years. He was buried
the same day in the Island of the Poplars, in the Lake

of Ermenonville, and there his ashes rested till the triumph of the Revolution, which he had done so much to bring about.[1] On the 11th of October, 1793, they were removed, amid a tumult of enthusiasm, to Paris, and placed in the Pantheon, over whose portal are inscribed the words: *Aux grands Hommes, la Patrie reconnaissante.*

This sketch of Rousseau's life, imperfect as it is, will enable us to form a conception and an estimate of his character and ideals, which underlie his social and educational theories.

We shall not greatly err, if we say that the foundation of Rousseau's character was spontaneity, that his whole life was an endeavor to give free and unconstrained expression to this, and that his works were so many efforts to champion it, as the ideal of life, and to show how it might be preserved, free from constraint and corruption. In Rousseau himself, this spontaneity, naturally very rich and strong, was fostered by an education which, leaving him at liberty to follow his momentary caprices, fired his imagination and made it ungovernable, so that he early became utterly incapable of submitting to any restraint, regulation, continuous occupation, or duty, however sacred. He lived in, and for, the present moment, seeking to draw from it the greatest amount of enjoyment, tranquil or ecstatic, as his mood happened to demand, without any thought of past, future, or the claims of others. He was too immediate to cherish

---

[1] **The report that he committed suicide seems utterly destitute of foundation. [Since this was written, an examination of his skull has placed this beyond doubt.]**

either love or hatred for absent things or persons. He was without malignity, because malignity causes discomfort; he loved for the pleasure love gave him, and when that ceased, love ceased. He was equally a stranger to revenge and gratitude. He could abandon his best friend, and then weep torrents of delicious tears over his or her forlorn condition. He could gush over his friends as long as they were willing merely to gush back; but, when they showed any signs of coldness, or tried to call him back to a sense of duty, he was ready to accuse them of the grossest ingratitude or blackest treachery. Knowing absolutely nothing of moral discipline, and having learnt none of those moral principles which render permanent and healthy social relations possible, he easily got disgusted with society, and was always ready to withdraw to solitude, which he could people with beings endowed with prodigal emotion, duly responsive to his own. For the same reason, while he exulted in virtue, when virtue was picturesque and pleasant, he was ready to give way to the basest of vices, if he could thereby obtain pleasure or avoid pain. He could never prevail upon himself to do anything that was disagreeable, no matter what law of duty imposed it upon him. He could wax eloquent on the duties of parents, and melt into tears at the sight of innocent children; yet he sent his own offspring to the foundling asylum. Such are some of the fruits of spontaneity.

But perhaps the most astonishing thing about Rousseau is, that he went through life, not only without learning the meaning of duty, but firmly believing that the life of pure spontaneity and caprice which he led was the ideal life, and that he himself was the best of men. This, indeed, he openly maintains. So far, indeed, was he from being ashamed of his undisciplined spontaneity, that he wrote his *Confessions* to prove that the spontaneous man is the best of men. We need not be surprised, then, to find that all his works are so many pleas for spontaneity, so many attempts to show all the evils which afflict humanity to be due to restraints placed upon spontaneity or attempts to discipline it; that they are so many schemes for making humanity blest, by the removal of these restraints. Indeed, it is hardly an exaggeration to say that the whole aim of Rousseau's literary activity is to show how men may be made happy and contented, without being obliged to become moral.

But what Rousseau sought to prove by eloquent words, by insidious appeals to man's natural craving for happiness on easy terms, he disproved by his own character, his actions, and the sad results of both. His character, with its obtrusive independence, due to absence of all acknowledgment of moral ties, is spongy, unmanly, and repellent. We might pity him, if he did not pity himself so much; but we can in no case admire or love him. His actions are merely so many efforts to obtain self-satisfaction, and that, too, of a purely sensuous, not to say sensual, sort. Though often imprudent, he is never heroic; though sentimentally or picturesquely kind, he is never generous or high-minded. If he submits to wrong, he does so more from sloth than from magnanimity. The results of his character and actions, of which his theories are but the generalized expression and defence, are a sufficient warning against such character, actions, and theories. These results were querulousness, misery, and insanity, unillumined by one ray of conscious heroism or moral worth. The man who had no other interest in life than the satisfaction of his own senses and emotions, found life meaningless, when satiety, abuse, and age had blunted these; and when, despite all unnatural stimulation from a diseased imagination, they became sources of pain, instead of sources of pleasure, nothing was left for him but spontaneous reactions in the form of querulousness, self-pity, and insanity. A sadder old age than Rousseau's is not often recorded.

As the above estimate of Rousseau's character may seem harsh and unsympathetic, it ought to be added that it is based entirely upon his own account of himself. In order to show this, it may be well to transcribe here a few passages from the four letters which he wrote to M. de Malesherbes, in January, 1762, in his best days, shortly before the publication of the *Social Contract* and *Émile:* —

"My heart cares too much for other attachments, to care so much for public opinion. I am too fond of my pleasure and my independence, to be as much the slave of vanity as they suppose. A man for whom fortune and the hope of a brilliant future never outweighed a rendezvous or a pleasant supper, is not likely to sacrifice his honor to the desire of being talked about." . . . "I was long mistaken as to the cause of my invincible disgust with human society." . . . "What, then, is this cause? It is simply this indomitable spirit of liberty, which nothing has been able to overcome, and before which fortune, honors, reputation even, are as nothing. Certain it is that this spirit of liberty is due less to pride than to indolence; but this indolence is incredible. Everything scares it; the smallest duties of civil life are insupportable to it; a word to speak, a letter to write, a visit to pay, as soon as they have to be done, are tortures to me. This is why, while ordinary intercourse with men is odious to me, friendship is so dear — because there is no duty about it. You follow your heart, and all is done. This also is why I have always dreaded kindnesses; for every kindness demands gratitude, and I feel my heart ungrateful, simply because gratitude is a duty. In a word, the kind of happiness I want consists, not so much in doing what I wish, as in not doing what I don't wish. Active life has no temptations for me. I had a thousand times rather do nothing than do anything against my will. I have a hundred times thought that I should not have been unhappy in the Bastille, having merely to stay there." . . . "An indolent soul, recoiling from all responsibilities, and an ardent, bilious temperament, easily affected and excessively sensitive to all that affects it, are two things which seem unlikely to meet in the same character; yet, contrary though they be, they form the basis of mine." . . . "My soul, alienated from itself, belongs wholly to my body; the disordered condition of my poor machine holds it every day more captive, until the time when the two shall part company altogether." . . . "My woes are the work of Nature; my happiness is my own work. Say what you will, I have been well-behaved, because I have been as happy as my nature allowed me to be. I have not looked for my happiness in the far distance, but in myself; and there I have found it." . . . "When my sufferings make me sadly measure the length of the nights, what period of my life do you suppose I recall most frequently and with most pleasure, in my dreams?" . . . "It is the period of my retreat, my solitary walks, the swift but delicious days I have passed all by myself, with my good, simple housekeeper, my beloved dog, my old cat, the birds of the field and the deer of the forest, the whole of nature and its inconceivable author. When, rising with the sun, in order to see him rise . . . I saw the approach of a fine day, my first wish was that neither letters nor visits would come to spoil its charm. After giving up the forenoon to different chores, all of which I did with pleasure, because I might have put them off till another time, I hastened to dine, in order to escape intruders, and secure a longer afternoon. By one o'clock, even in the hottest days, I set out." ... "When once I had turned a certain corner, with what palpitation of heart, with what flashes of joy, I began to breathe, feeling myself safe, and saying: 'Here I am, my own master for the rest of the day!' Then I went along more quietly to find some wilderness, where nothing showing the hand of man bore witness to servitude or mastership, some retreat into which I could suppose I had been the first to penetrate, and where no third intruder could come between Nature and me. It was there that she seemed to display an ever new splendor before me." ... "My imagination did not long leave unpeopled the land thus adorned. I soon peopled it with beings according to my own heart, and, driving far away opinion, prejudice, and all factitious passions, I brought into the retreats of Nature men worthy to inhabit them. I formed them into a delightful society, of which I did not feel myself unworthy to be a member; I made a Golden Age, to please myself; and, filling these beautiful days with all those scenes in my life which had left behind pleasant recollections, and with all those which my heart could still desire, I melted into tears over the true pleasures of humanity, pleasures which are so delicious and so pure, and henceforth so far from men! Oh, if in these moments my dreams were broken by any idea of Paris, of my time, of my little literary aureole, with what disdain did I at once send it flying, in order to give myself up, without distraction, to the exquisite feelings which filled my soul! Nevertheless, in the midst of all this, I confess, the unreality of my chimeras sometimes suddenly saddened me. If my dreams had all turned into realities, they would not have satisfied me. I should still have imagined, dreamed, desired. I found in myself an inexplicable void, which nothing could fill, a certain rising of the heart toward another sort of enjoyment, of which I had no idea, but yet of which I felt the need." ... "I will not hide from you that, notwithstanding my consciousness of my vices, I hold myself in high esteem."

Such was the man who undertook to be the educator of his kind!

CHAPTER IV

ROUSSEAU'S SOCIAL THEORIES

> The State is prior to the individual.
> ARISTOTLE, *Politics.*

> All men are equally by nature free.
> HOBBES, *Leviathan*, Cap. XXI.

> All public regimen, of what kind soever, seemeth evidently to have risen from the deliberate advice, consultation, and composition between men, judging it convenient and behoveful, there being no impossibility in Nature, considered by itself, but that man might have lived without any public regimen.
> HOOKER, *Ecclesiastical Polity*, Bk. I., § 10.

> Love thou thy land, with love far-brought
> From out the storied Past, and used
> Within the Present, but transfused
> Through future time by power of thought.
>
> *   *   *   *   *   *
>
> But pamper not a hasty time,
> Nor feed with crude imaginings
> The herd, wild hearts and feeble wings
> That every sophister can lime.
> TENNYSON.

ROUSSEAU, in his second letter to M. de Malesherbes, tells us that his discourse on the Sciences and Arts, that on the Origin of Inequality among Men, and *Émile*, are "three inseparable works, which together form a single whole." He ought to have added, as a fourth, the *Social Contract;* but it was not then published, though written, and he had his reasons for not speaking of it. Since it is thus impossible to understand his educational theory, as laid down in *Émile*, without having first grasped his social and political doctrines, as expounded in the other three, we must now consider these works.

We have already, in Chapter I., briefly traced the course of the reaction against the theocentric, authoritative teachings and institutions of the Middle Age, in favor of that anthropocentric, autonomous individualism which is the distinguishing characteristic of recent times, and have seen how the source of political authority was gradually transferred from the inscrutable will of God, supernaturally revealed, and embodied in kings and princes, to the manifold minds and wills of men. We have further seen that, when the question came to be asked: How did these minds and wills, being manifold and discordant, produce an authority which they are all bound to acknowledge? the answer was, Through a Social Contract, by which men voluntarily agreed to defend the rights which had previously belonged to them in the state of Nature. Finally, we have seen that, while at first this contract was believed to be irrevocable, and the sovereign, once chosen, to be, through succession, perpetual and absolute, this belief gradually gave place to another, according to which the contract with the sovereign [1] might at any time be annulled or altered

[1] We must always distinguish between the Social Contract proper, which is an agreement among men to submit to a sovereign (composed of one person or many), from the contract with the sovereign elected. The latter is the institution of government; **the former is the creation of a state or commonwealth. Rousseau, unlike Locke, is clear enough on this point.**

by the will of the people, and the sovereign deposed. Thus the conviction gradually grew up that men, instead of being the creatures and slaves of institutions, are their creators and masters; that institutions exist for men, and not men for institutions, which should, accordingly, be modified to suit them. Thus, man and his desires became the ultimate end to which institutions, like all other things, are but means. It required but one unguarded step to pass from this to the notion that institutions are mere arrangements for enabling each individual man to give free play to his natural impulses — his animal spontaneity — without fear of being interrupted or disturbed.[1] Rousseau took this step, and upon the notion so reached built up his political, social, and educational theories. They are all attempts to answer the question: How is it possible, through social institutions, which, under certain circumstances, become a painful necessity, for man's natural spontaneity, wherein consists his happiness, to find unthwarted expression? This, indeed, is the question which Rousseau supposed he was answering; but, as a matter of fact, he went a step further, and asked, instead: How would social institutions have to be arranged in order that *my* spontaneity might have free expression? Now, as we have seen (Chapters II., III.), Rousseau's spontaneity was both excessive and peculiar. He was almost the last man to be adopted as the type of men in general, and this he knew very well.[2] He belonged, indeed,

[1] This was exactly the Sophists' position, which **Socrates triumphantly refuted.** See my *Aristotle*, pp. 100 sqq.

[2] See the opening sentences of the *Confessions*.

to the very numerous class of self-centred, unenterprising dalliers; but he was an extreme and, therefore, a rare specimen of it. Being, according to his own admission, at once ardently sensuous and hopelessly indolent, he craved those kinds of half-animal enjoyment that could be attained with the smallest amount of reflection, will, and physical energy. Hence, his ideal was a quiet, simple, easy-going life, with no duties and no aims, with plenty of time for dallying, dreaming, and love-making, and with the hope of a divinely provided future eternity of the same sort. He desired above all things to feel, and to avoid the trouble of thinking or acting.[1] With the story of Eden and the theories of Hobbes and Locke in his mind, he was fain to believe that this was man's natural condition; but, instead of holding with these that men had risen, by combining into societies through a rational contract, he maintained that they had fallen, and that thought and knowledge were evidences of depravity. To prove this, and to recommend a return to Nature and savagery, was the aim of his two discourses; while, in the *Social Contract*, he tried to rescue as much of "Nature" as he could, in the midst of Culture. Still deep in mediæval notions, he had no conception of evolution through struggle, or of the only blessedness worthy of man, — the consciousness of continual moral victory in such struggle.

[1] He never did either except under the influence of passion. Hume said of him, "He has only *felt* during the whole course of his life, and in this respect his sensibility rises to a pitch, beyond what I have seen any example of; but it still gives him a more acute feeling of pain than of pleasure." Quoted in Morley's *Rousseau*, Vol. II., p. 299.

Bearing these facts in mind, we have no difficulty in realizing the perturbation caused in Rousseau's unstable nature by the Dijon Academy's question, which called forth his first discourse. He believed, with all his heart,[1] that not only art and science, but everything that presupposes discipline and continuous thought or labor, was prejudicial to morals, that is, to the sort of life he coveted; and he undertook to show this by an appeal to present experience and past history. Having, in his contact with men, learnt what all of us learn, — that the external polish of manners and the elegant accomplishments which earn for a man the character of gentleman, and make him a social favorite, are not only compatible, but frequently coexist, with inner meanness, heartlessness, vulgarity, and treachery, whereas rusticity of manners and slowness of intellect often conceal an inner core of sterling gentlemanliness and worth, — he jumps to the conclusion that polish and culture, by furnishing a uniform style of mask for the virtuous and the vicious alike, make all human intercourse a mere masquerade, destroy simplicity, and so corrupt society. This conclusion he finds confirmed by a survey of the ancient nations, which he affirms, with a fair show of truth, to have been virtuous, strong, and progressive as long as they were ignorant of the sciences and arts, and to have declined from the moment when these were introduced. Though admitting that great thinkers and artists may be useful, if they are

---

[1] One thing about Rousseau can never be doubted, — and it is a great thing, and due to his spontaneity, — his complete emotional sincerity. His desires were very real to him.

also great and virtuous citizens, like Cicero and Bacon, he has only scorn for the ordinary run of philosophers, scientists, and literary panderers to popular taste, bewailing, as an almost unmixed evil, the invention of printing, which makes it possible to perpetuate their productions. Expressed briefly, his argument is, that scientific and artistic culture is incompatible with virtue. He concludes that such culture should be eschewed, and men return to the simplicity of primitive life and blissful ignorance, unprovocative of ambition.

Paradoxical and untenable as Rousseau's general position is, it contains a large amount of truth, which won it adherents in an age of universal unreality, hypocrisy, and corruption, masked by politeness. It is true that polish without virtue, gentlemanly bearing without generosity and sympathy, erudition without insight, brilliancy without earnestness, and charity without self-sacrifice, are evil and not good. It is true that mere occupation with science for science' sake, without any sense of its relation to moral life, and with art for the sake of the passive pleasure it yields, is a sure sign of moral decadence and national enfeeblement. It is true that that culture alone is good which leads to lofty simplicity and robust virtue. It was no small merit on the part of Rousseau to have given these truths energetic expression; but, when he confounded true culture of mind, affection, and will with mere superficial polish, and refined simplicity with ignorant savagery or rusticity, he was misleading the world and defeating his own ends, by a display of that hollow and pernicious rhetoric which he so heartily despised and stigmatized.

Rousseau's first discourse was attacked from many quarters; but this by no means daunted him. His passions being concerned, he not only replied to all objectors, but returned to the charge with fresh ammunition in his second discourse, in which he sought to answer the question: *What is the Origin of Inequality among Men, and is it authorized by the Natural Law?* In this, true to his love of feeling and his hatred of thinking, and mindful of his lonely, sensuous reveries in the forest of Montmorency, he assures us that "the state of reflection is a state contrary to Nature, and the man who thinks is a depraved animal." He draws a picture of man in his purely animal state, when he "wandered in the forests, without industry, without speech, without home, without war or tie, with no need of his fellows and no desire to hurt them, perhaps even not knowing any one of them individually." Being endowed with the sentiment of pity, he was naturally kind and good, inclined rather to help than to hurt his fellows when they came in his way; and, as there was as yet no inequality, he had no ground for hatred, envy, pride, or any of the numerous vices that follow in their train. Following Nature, he was free, strong, and happy.

Rousseau next proceeds to show how, as men, multiplying, found more and more difficulty in obtaining food, they invented traps and similar devices, and so began to have private property, and how, finally, learning that they could accomplish their ends better by combining, they entered first into momentary, and then into permanent, relations with each other. With the rise of the latter, they began to settle together, to build themselves huts, and to have their families about them. Division of labor began, and with it a certain loss of robust, savage courage. Civilization was beginning, and with it corruption. Still, as there was yet no marked inequality, there was almost no vice, and, indeed, this was perhaps the happiest of all human conditions. The great evil of inequality began when what had previously been common to all, was claimed as private property. "The first man who, having enclosed a piece of land, took upon him to say, 'This is mine,' and found people simple enough to believe him, was the true founder of civil society. How many crimes, wars, murders, miseries, horrors, would have been spared the human race by him who, tearing up the stakes, or filling up the ditch, should have called out to his fellows: 'Beware of listening to this impostor! You are lost, if you forget that the fruit belongs to all, the earth to none!'" From this point on, it is easy to follow the development of civil society, involving, as it does, the decay of freedom, virtue, and happiness, and the growth of slavery, vice, and misery. "If we follow the progress of inequality," he says, ". . . we shall find that the establishment of law and of the right of private property was its first term; the institution of magistracy, its second; and the third and last, the transition from legitimate to arbitrary power; so that the condition of rich and poor was authorized by the first epoch; that of strong and weak, by the second; and by the third, that of master and slave, which is the last degree of inequality, and the one to which all the others finally come." And Rousseau draws a picture of civilized society, which contrasts luridly enough with his previous picture of the life of the "noble savage." The conclusion is, that all inequality among men is due to private property, and all vice, misery, and slavery to inequality. The moral, of course, is, Return to savage life — to the state of Nature.

No better commentary can be made on this book than the one which Voltaire made, in the letter in which he thanked the author for a copy of it. "I have received," he says, "your new book against the human race, and return you my thanks. Never was such ability put forth in the endeavor to make us all stupid. On reading your book, one longs to walk on all fours." The work, regarded as a whole, is indeed the height of absurdity; and yet it contains a large amount of solid truth, and produced, in the practical world, effects which determined, and are still determining, the fate of nations. What the author says in regard to the origin of language and of ideas is better than anything that had been said before him. His views on the relations of property to social life and ethics are more and more coming to be recognized as true. His notions of the relation of thought to reality, if they had been worked out into a system, would have given us a saner and truer philosophy than any that has ever appeared.[1] And the book

[1] Take, for example, the following: "The human understanding owes much to the passions, which, by common consent, likewise owe much to it. It is through their activity that our reason perfects itself; we seek to know only because we desire to enjoy; and it is impossible to conceive how a being having neither desires nor fears should take the trouble to reason. The passions, on the other hand, originate in our needs, and their progress in our knowledge."

contains not only the tinder that kindled the French Revolution, and the germ that burst into the American Declaration of Independence, but also the forces of all those deeper and more pervasive movements that are "toiling in the gloom," under the surface of our present social order, — socialism, anarchism, nihilism, and the like. Lastly, there is in the book an important pedagogical truth, which may be summed up in the Greek aphorism: Education is learning to love and hate correctly.

The second discourse was written in 1753; nine years later appeared the *Social Contract*, meant to be merely a portion of a larger work on *Political Institutions*. Rousseau having, meanwhile, come to recognize that a return to the state of Nature is impossible, that civil society and culture have come to stay, now proposed to himself this problem: *To find a form of association which shall defend, with all the common force, the person and property of each associate, and through which each, uniting with all, shall, nevertheless, obey only himself, and remain as free as before.* In other words, he wished to discover how the freedom lost

---

Had these thoughts been heeded, Kant would have been saved from his dualism between the matter and form of thought; and the world would have been spared the whole laborious and futile attempt of idealism to build up a real world out of the forms or categories of thought. We shall never get a philosophy worthy of the name, until, with Rousseau, we see that all reality is feeling, and that thought is merely the articulation of feeling. Feeling, in the form of desire, is the ideal; in the form of satisfaction, the actual. The history of the categories of thought is the history of all evolution; not because the categories unfold themselves, but because desire, in its effort toward ever fuller and more varied satisfaction, differentiates itself into them.

with the state of Nature might be recovered in the state of Culture. His answer was, By means of a Social Contract of this form: "Each of us places in a common stock his person and all his power, under the supreme direction of the general will, and we further receive each member as an individual part of the whole." In other words, men, coming to recognize that "they had reached a point where the obstacles to their preservation in a state of Nature were too much for the forces which each individual could put forth to maintain himself in that state," and that, therefore, they must perish if they tried to continue in it, resolved to unite their forces in order to overcome these obstacles. In this way, they gave up their individual freedom and accepted, in exchange, social freedom; that is, such freedom as is possible when each individual submits himself to rules reached through a compromise between the wills of all. Whereas, previously, each individual was a sovereign in his own right, now the only sovereign is the whole of society, of which each individual is a member. Or, to put it otherwise, men, to escape complete bondage to Nature, accepted partial bondage to society, in which each will is free only in so far as it is a part of the general will, influencing all and being influenced by all. This will, in any particular case, is found in the vote of the majority. Of course, this social freedom, according to Rousseau, is not an equivalent for natural freedom, which should be preserved wherever it is possible; but it is the next best thing. Only, care must be taken that it does not, as at present, degenerate into tyranny on the one hand and slavery on the other.[1] Though the authority of the sovereign is absolute, inalienable, indivisible, and the source of all laws, yet, since the execution of laws must be entrusted by law to a part of the sovereign, there is always danger that this part, though possessing no independent authority, will either use the laws for its own benefit or act contrary to the laws, and thus enslave the other part. When this happens, the Social Contract is broken, and the parties to it return to a state of Nature, free from all authority, but free, at the same time, to make a fresh contract. Here we have at once the conditions and the justification of revolution.

Such, in very brief form, is the main gist of the Social Contract, which has played such a dissolvent part in the history of the last hundred years. It is, from our present point of view, easy to criticise it, but it is also easy to misunderstand its main thesis. It may be, and is, true that Rousseau conceives all social order to rest upon an original compact, made in the distant past; but this is as good as irrelevant to his purpose. His book is meant to solve a problem, not to reason from a fact. His contention is, that all the relations of the individual to society ought, *at every moment*, to be such as would result from a free contract entered into by persons all enjoying the same natural rights, all free and all equal, on the understanding that all these rights should be maintained, and that all the contractants should re-

[1] "Man is born free, and is everywhere in chains." These are the opening words of the first chapter of the *Social Contract*.

main free and equal under the contract. Is this true? that is the question. It is not.

Starting from false premises, Rousseau naturally arrived at false conclusions. His "state of Nature" is a pure fiction of the imagination. Man, in such a state, would not be man at all; for all that makes him man is evolved through association. He is not born free; for freedom and slavery are terms that have no meaning except in a social order. Animal caprice is not freedom. Man does not lose, but gain, freedom by association, and the more extensive the association the greater the freedom. The phrase "natural rights," which has played so mischievous a part in thought and practice since Rousseau's day, is actually self-contradictory, or, as logicians say, contains a *contradictio in adjecto*. Where there is no social order, there are no rights at all; in so far, all beings are equal. Rights imply duties, and both imply mutuality, which involves association. Society is not due to an agreement whereby men pool rights previously and independently possessed; it is a combination whereby rights are created. If we insist upon giving a meaning to the phrase "natural rights," it must be those rights which a man, born into a society already constituted, may fairly claim, on the ground that certain duties are demanded of him, even though he has had no voice in the organization of that society. At the present day, when all men are held to be born into human society,[1] and therefore to have certain duties, all are held to have *such* natural

[1] Aristotle was far wiser than Rousseau, when he said, "Man is *by nature* a political animal."

rights. But this view is of very recent origin, even in the most civilized countries.

Again, "general will" is a nonsensical phrase; for will is always individual, and, even if we substitute "aggregate of individual wills," this aggregate is not found by pairing off, and setting aside, opposing wills, and counting only those that can find none to pair off with. One will does not cancel another, however much it may be opposed to it. But Rousseau's chief error lay in this, that, like Plato, the first and greatest of Utopians, he supposed that human nature could be suddenly transformed by the fiat of the legislator, and society be made to assume any arrangement which he, with his geometrical wisdom or landscape-gardening fancy, might choose to give it. Neither of these men based his theories upon a careful study of human nature and progress, or inquired what, given humanity such as it is, with its ignorance, caprice, and wilfulness, was possible for it at any given stage in its career. Both of them set out with their own feelings and preferences, and, finding that these were thwarted and confined by the social order about them, went to work, with their imaginations, to construct another, in which these feelings and preferences should have full play. This is the fatal vice of all Utopians and sentimentalists. They make the satisfaction of their own needs and imaginary desires the aim of social endeavor, forgetting the homely proverbs, that "you cannot make a silk purse out of a sow's ear," and that "one man's meat is another man's poison." Moreover, since all sentimentalists belong to the dalliant class (see p. 24), they are always trying to make arrangements for dalliance, that is, for the cessation of struggle and energetic enterprise, and for the realization of an earthly paradise of sweet rest and dreamy emotions. They cannot be made to see that all true life is struggle, and that, if the struggle should cease, life would cease to have any value, and become a mere opium-eater's dream.

But it is the very vice of these subjective Utopians that wins fanatical adherents for their theories; for the fanatic is simply the man who, by calling the imagined satisfaction of his own desires the sacred ideal of humanity, can proclaim it, without fear or shame, to the whole world, and, in words fledged with passion and tipped with sympathetic poison, call upon it to aid him in giving it reality, not hesitating, if the opportunity occurs, to employ, in the process, fire, sword, gibbet, or guillotine. If he is of the extreme sort, he will announce that he speaks with the voice of God, and command all men to believe in him and follow his lead, on pain of eternal torture. Thus did Muhammad, Joseph Smith, and "the Bâb" of modern Persia.

As the virus of Rousseau's social theories, of which his educational system confessedly forms a part, has not yet ceased to poison the minds of men and women of the dalliant order, it may be well to bring out here the nature of this virus, and to show its pernicious effects in social life.

A rapid glance at the world, as we know it, suffices to show us that it is composed of clusters of feelings, distinguished, grouped, and generalized into things, by what we call the categories of thought. Matter,[1] force, love, hate, self, are feelings, differentiated by time, space, relation, and the like. If, now, we follow the course of evolution, as revealed to us by recent investigation, we shall see that it is a progress in feeling from indistinction to distinction, from unconsciousness to consciousness, and, finally, to self-consciousness, which appears to be the ultimate distinctness. To this last, man alone, so far as we know, has attained, and even he has not attained to it completely. He is still "half-akin to brute,"[2] still swayed by impulses which he is not able to differentiate, analyze, or make completely subservient to his ultimate end. His passions — even his love and pity — are, to a large extent, still blind, and he acts from motives whose rationality he often does not see. In like manner, his social relations are still half instinctive, being due, not to conscious contract, but to use and wont. He thus finds himself in a certain status, which, if one wishes to abuse language, may be called thraldom, or even slavery, but which, in fact, is merely the natural condition of all beings that have not, as the result of complete self-consciousness, attained perfect self-determination. It is a familiar saying that all social advance is from status to contract,[3] which means from relations contracted through instinct, use, and wont, to relations entered into with a conscious purpose. Since this advance cannot reach

---

[1] If we abstract from matter what is plainly feeling, *e.g.* shape, color, hardness, impenetrability, there is nothing left. Matter is a group of feelings. See Huxley, *Descartes' Discourse touching the Method of using one's Reason*, pp. 373 sq.

[2] Tennyson, *In Memoriam*, epilogue.

[3] See Sir H. S. Maine, *Ancient Law*, pp. 165 sq.

its goal until men, grown completely self-conscious, can undertake to conduct their lives in view of an all-embracing, freely-set purpose, it is evident that a social contract in Rousseau's sense, a contract extending to all the relations of life, can come only at the end, and by no means at the beginning, of social life. It is the failure to grasp this simple result of historic induction that makes it possible seriously to construct Utopias and, at the same time, makes their failure almost certain. An Utopia is simply a proposal to impose one man's notion of the conditions that would insure his happiness upon his fellows, an arrangement which, instead of securing their freedom, would completely enthral them. Every Utopian, from Plato down, places himself in the ruling class. Imagine how Rousseau would feel as a member of the warrior class in Plato's Republic, or as an operative in Mr. Bellamy's industrial commonwealth! In all history, we know but of one man who succeeded in imposing his private ideal upon his race and, through it, upon a large portion of the world; and that was Muhammad; but we must not forget that he did so by means of supernatural claims, and that the results have been fanaticism and slavery.[1]

---

[1] Rousseau has some excellent remarks on the efforts of Peter the Great to force his ideal upon Russia. "The Russians," he says, "will never be truly civilized, because they were so too soon. Peter had an imitative genius: he had not true genius, such as creates and makes everything out of nothing. Some of the things he did were good; the greater part were ill-timed. He saw that his people was barbarian; he did not see that it was not ripe for civilization. He tried to civilize it, when he ought to have inured it to war. He wished at once to make Germans and Englishmen, when he ought to have begun by making Russians. He

No good can ever be done to a people by trying to force it into any mould prepared for it from without. Even if for a time it submits to the mould, it will, sooner or later, either burst it or perish through cramping. In a healthy state, peoples feel their way forward, so to speak, spontaneously, forming new ideals at every step, and freely realizing them at the next. All that the enthusiastic lover of his kind, the wise reformer, can do, is to hasten this process by diffusing such knowledge and culture as shall give a deeper and wider meaning to experience, and so make possible higher ideals. Any attempt to force the process, or to substitute for its slowly, but freely, attained results, a rigid, unprogressive scheme, such as Utopias are sure to be, can lead to nothing but slavery and death. Equally fatal to liberty and well-being are all attempts to induce a people to alter its whole social system in favor of some scheme that seems to promise greater material prosperity, greater ease, comfort, and dalliance. This is the mistake made by the socialists and many other well-meaning, but ill-advised, reformers of the present day. This was the mistake made by Rousseau, whose *Social Contract* may be said to be the bible of both socialism and anarchism.[1] Holding that the bonds of civil society were, or might be, created by a contract, he concluded that they were dissolved when the terms of that contract were violated, and that thereupon the contract-

prevented his subjects from becoming what they might have been, by persuading them that they were what they were not. . . . The Russian empire will try to subjugate Europe, and will itself be subjugated."

[1] See below, Cap. XI.

ants or their representatives could revert to their original condition of savage individualism, with freedom to slay each other to their heart's content, and, when tired of that, to return — a battered remnant — to civic life, by making a new contract to suit their tastes. The premise of this argument being false, the conclusion was necessarily so likewise; but this was not the worst. Rousseau forgot three most important things: (1) to state the precise terms of the social contract; (2) to determine what would constitute a violation of these terms; (3) to say who should have the right of declaring authoritatively when they were violated. On his principles it would be entirely competent for any body of men, at any time, to declare the contract broken, and to revert to anarchy.

Thus the *Social Contract* is mistaken in theory, and pernicious, or impossible, in practice. It rests upon a false conception of human nature and its laws, and places, as a fact, at the beginning of social evolution, what can only be an ideal to be gradually approached as an end. It places the perfection of human nature in a condition of savage isolation, governed by pure caprice, and regards all advance toward moral liberty, through social organization, as a decline and a degeneration. It makes liberty and equality conditions prior and external to civilization, instead of, as they are, the highest results of the social process. It teaches men to regard social restraints and institutions as something artificial and conventional, which it is their duty to cast aside, whenever they can, in favor of savage freedom, with its animal immediateness and spontaneity. If it reluctantly admits the necessity of a social order, it regards this, not as a means of moral training in conscious self-control, which is true freedom, but as a contrivance for conserving animal spontaneity and caprice.

From Rousseau's views regarding the truly important in life and the value of social organization, we can easily divine the character of his educational system. With that we shall begin to deal in the next chapter.

CHAPTER V

ROUSSEAU'S EDUCATIONAL THEORIES

INFANCY

(*Émile*, Bk. I.)

To live alone, one must be a god or a beast.
ARISTOTLE, *Politics*.

An illustrious author says that it is only the bad man that is alone. I say it is only the good man that is alone.
ROUSSEAU, *Émile*, Bk. II.

The whole universe can be only a point for an oyster.
Ibid.

WE have seen that Rousseau's social and political theories had their origin in two things: (1) a group of notions, of naturalistic and individualistic tendency, current in his day; (2) his own sensuous, indolent, dalliant nature, which continually craved a life of bovine satisfaction, unencumbered by thought, or sense of duty. Seizing upon the distinction between natural and civic life, and temperamentally hating the latter, he proceeded, in direct opposition to Hobbes and Locke, to decry it, as slavish and depraved, and to glorify the former, as alone free and healthy. In a word, he set up his own dreams of dalliance as the ideal of human life. Such a course will always be open and tempting to men of his impatient, undisciplined character, so long as we persist in drawing a hard and fast distinction between the life of Nature and the life of Culture, and, failing to see that they are simply two commergent stages in one process, attribute them to different principles. It is always perilous to introduce any sort of dualism into existence, or to seek for the explanation of the lower forms of it elsewhere than in the laws manifested in the higher. If we cannot show that ethical life is natural, we can, at least, show that natural life is rudimentarily ethical. Thus viewed, the lower manifestation will hardly be preferred to the higher. No errors are so fatally mischievous as metaphysical errors. To one such error were due most of the horrors of the French Revolution.

For a century preceding Rousseau's time, educational theories had been rife in a world awakening from the lurid, Dantesque dreams of the Middle Age. The old belief, that man's nature is fallen and depraved, had gradually been replaced by a belief that it is fundamentally sound and good; and, at the same time, education had come to be regarded, not as a means of eradicating vile human nature, and replacing it by a new divine nature, but as a means of developing human nature itself. In England, Locke had written a plain, common-sense treatise on education[1] from the latter point of view, and from this Rousseau drew his chief inspiration. About 1760 the Jesuits, who had done so much to promote education of the repressive and eradicative sort, were losing their hold,[2] and thus an opportunity was offered for educational theories and practices of the opposite kind.

[1] *Some Thoughts concerning Education* (1688)
[2] They were expelled from France in 1764.

Of this Rousseau, among others, took advantage, and, in 1762, produced *Émile*, which assumes that all education ought to be the development of Nature.

Rousseau's educational system was meant to be a preparation for that sort of life which his own nature pictured to him as the highest — a quiet, uneventful, unreflective, half-animal, half-childish "natural" life, free from serious tasks, aims, or duties, — the life of a savage, conceived as sensitive and capricious, but kind and lazy.[1] Had he been logical, he would have simply advised parents to send their children at birth, for nurture and education, to a tribe of savages or nomads, as the Meccans are said to have done in the time of Muhammad. But, logicality not being one of his virtues, he propounded this problem: (How can a child, born in civil society, be so reared as to remain unaffected and uncorrupted by the vices inseparable from civilization? His solution is *Émile*. In this work, education is conceived as a negative, protective process, warding off external evil, that the good native to the child[2] may be free to unfold itself, in all its

[1] Savage life, as conceived by Rousseau, is mainly the product of his own imagination. His ideal savage is simply himself.

[2] Wordsworth was under the sentimental glamor of Rousseau's influence, when he wrote, in his *Ode to Immortality*, the incautious, flattering lines: —

> "Not in entire forgetfulness,
> And not in utter nakedness;
> But trailing clouds of glory do we come
> From God, who is our home."

And so was Lowell, when he wrote: —

> "All that hath been majestical
> In life or death, since time began,
> Is native in the simple heart of all,
> The angel heart of man."
>
> *An Incident in a Railroad Car.*

spontaneity. It will be the proper time to consider the justice of this conception after we have examined the work in detail.

Rousseau flaunts his colors from the outset. The opening words of the first book of *Émile* are: "Everything is well, as it comes from the hands of the Author of things; everything degenerates in the hands of man." Here a strong line is drawn between Nature, as the work of God, and Art, or Culture, as the work of man, and the latter, instead of being conceived, as Shakespeare and Hobbes conceived it, as the continuation and crown of the former, is regarded as something meanly opposing and thwarting it.[1] Man distorts and disfigures everything, and, indeed, if he is to live in society, he must do so; for only distorted men can so live. "In the condition which things have now reached, a man left to himself, in the midst of others, at his birth, would be the most disfigured of all. Prejudices, authority, necessity, example, all the social institutions in which we find ourselves submerged, would stifle Nature in him, without putting anything in its place." To prevent this, "the springing shrub must be protected from the shock of human opinions," by education. "This education comes to us from Nature, or men, or things.[2] The internal development of our faculties and organs is due to Nature; the use which we are taught to make of this development is the education by men; and the

---

[1] See p. 9, and note, and compare the soliloquy of Edmund, in *King Lear*, Act I., sc. ii. Edmund is, indeed, the natural man, whose character Rousseau might have studied with advantage.

[2] Cf. my *Aristotle*, in this series, pp. 9 sqq.

acquisition of our own experience, through the objects which affect us, is the education by things."[1] A complete education is possible only when these three kinds of education are in harmony. "Now, . . . that by Nature does not depend upon us; that by things depends only in certain respects; that by men is the only one of which we are really masters." It follows that, since the first two cannot be conformed to the third, the third must be conformed to them, if there is to be harmony. Men, in endeavoring to impart education, must conform to the methods of Nature and things, which exert resistance but never authority. Hence, all authority must be excluded from methods of education. Ignoring things, Rousseau maintains that all education must conform to Nature. But what is Nature? It is the sum of man's instinctive or spontaneous tendencies, before they are altered by opinion or reflection. Education, therefore, must conform to these tendencies, and would do so, if its only aim were to produce men out of all relations to other men: But what are we to do, when, instead of educating man for himself, we wish to educate him for others? Then harmony is impossible. "Compelled to oppose either Nature or social institutions, we must choose between the man and the citizen; for we cannot make both at the same time." . . . "The natural man is all for himself:[2] he is the numerical unit, the absolute integer, having no relations save to himself

---

[1] This is a false classification. Our experience extends to Nature and man, as well as to things.

[2] See Dante, *Hell*, III., 22–69, where the lot of those who "were for themselves" (*per sè foro*) is forcibly depicted.

and his equal. The civil man is but a fractional unit, depending on its denominator, and deriving its value from its relation to the integer, which is the body social. Good social institutions are those which best understand how to disnature man, to take away his absolute existence and give him in exchange a relative one, transferring his *ego* to the common unit; so that each individual thinks himself no longer a one, but a part of the unit, and is sensible only in the whole."

Holding that education for manhood and education for citizenship are altogether incompatible, Rousseau insists that we must frankly choose between the two, otherwise we shall make "one of the men of the present day, a Frenchman, an Englishman, a bourgeois — a nothing." "The choice," he adds, "is not difficult to make; for at the present day there is neither country, nor citizen, nor public institution for educating citizens."[1] There remains only family education, or the education by Nature. Though aware that this will not qualify for civic functions, Rousseau, nevertheless, proposes to adopt it, on the ground that it will restore the natural, unsophisticated man, whose sole function is to be a man, "and that whoever is well trained for that, cannot fail to perform those which are related to it. Whether my pupil be intended for the

[1] This is just as true of our time as it was of Rousseau's, and he is in part to blame for the fact. We make the same unwise distinction between Nature and Culture, between man and citizen, that he did, as if Culture were not "an art that Nature makes," and as if citizenship were not an essential function of man, as man! We cannot possibly educate a man, as man, without educating him as a citizen.

army, the church, or the bar, is of small consequence. Prior to the calling of his family, Nature calls him to human life. To live is the craft I desire to teach him. When he leaves my hands, I admit he will be neither magistrate, soldier, nor priest; he will be, first of all, a man; all that a man may be, he will be able to be, as well as any one. Whatever changes Fortune may have in store for him, he will always be in his place."[1] "To live," according to Rousseau, "is not to breathe; it is to act, to use our organs, our senses, our faculties, and all the parts of us that give us the feeling of our existence. The man who has lived most is not he who has counted the greatest number of years, but he who has felt life most."[2]

Rousseau, then, undertakes to train men to live, that is, to enjoy the maximum of feeling, with as little

[1] Rousseau everywhere fails to distinguish between those social functions which are essential to man as man — family duties, citizenship — from those which are not, such as particular crafts and professions. It is not incumbent upon every man to be a blacksmith or a physician, but it is incumbent on every one to be a good citizen. This failure vitiates his entire educational system, and has led to serious practical consequences.

[2] This is another of Rousseau's cardinal errors. He makes life consist in feeling, but forgets that all the distinctness, variety, and wealth of feeling are due to intellectual categories. Without these, feeling, if it were anything, would be, at best, but a vague, meaningless stirring. Rousseau was led into this error by the prevalent thought of his time, which divorced ideas from sensible things, and tried to construct a dogmatic system out of them, as so divorced. Hume and Kant partly put an end to this kind of thought; but the world has been slow to find it out. The truth is, that the man who lives most, is he who most completely translates feeling (which includes sensation and desire) into thought and will, and thus rises above animality and instinct. Feeling is but seed-life. The "tree of life," of which whoso eats lives forever, is made up of knowledge and will, continuous thought, and moral self-direction and restraint.

reflection and restraint as may be.[1] In dealing with
the earliest years of the child's life, when undifferentiated feeling and desire predominate, he lays down
many sensible, mostly negative, rules. The young
child is not to be swaddled, confined, or rocked, but
to be allowed the utmost freedom of limb and voice;
it is to be nursed and tended by its mother, and not
by a hired nurse, and exposed to a reasonable amount
of heat, cold, and risk, in order that it may become
robust and courageous. Its cries must be attended to
at once, in so far as they express real needs, but no
further. If it wilfully uses crying in order to obtain
what it wants, but does not need, it must neither be
awed into silence nor indulged. In the former case
it will learn to submit to authority, in the latter, to
exercise it. "A child spends six or seven years in
this way, in the hands of women, a victim of their
caprices or of his own, and . . . after Nature has
been stifled by passions artificially created, this factitious creature is turned over to a tutor, who completes the development of the artificial germs which
he finds already formed, and who teaches him everything except to know himself, to make the most of
himself, to live and make himself happy.[2] Finally,
when this slavish and tyrannical child, crammed

---

[1] Cf. Gœthe, *Faust*, Pt. I., lines 38–50. The passage is quoted on p. 113. *Faust* is everywhere a protest against the teaching of Rousseau, represented by Mephistopheles.

[2] Happiness, or what we call "a good time," Rousseau desired, above all things, for himself, and, therefore, for children — which was the surest way not to get it, as he discovered to his cost. Happiness, as such, can never be a true or worthy human aim. See the closing sections of *Romola*.

with knowledge and devoid of sense, as weak of body as of soul, is thrown into the world, to display his ineptitude, his pride, and all his vices, he makes us deplore human misery and perversity. But we are mistaken: he is the child of our whims. Nature's child is quite different."

But how is this sad result to be avoided? Rousseau answers: "Stand guard over him from the moment he comes into the world. Take possession of him, and do not leave him till he is a man. You will not succeed otherwise." Father and mother, as the natural tutor and nurse, must combine all their efforts to develop the nature of the child. And Rousseau says some admirable and much-needed things on the duty of parents in this respect. The bosom of the family is the proper place for early education, and there is no more sacred or delightful duty than that of educating children. "A father, when he begets and feeds his children, performs but one-third of his task. He owes men to his kind, sociable men to society, citizens to the state. Every man who can pay this triple debt, and fails to do so, is culpable, and perhaps more culpable when he half pays it. Neither poverty, nor work, nor any human consideration relieves a man from the duty of rearing and educating his children himself. Reader, you may take my word for it: I warn every one who has a heart and neglects such sacred duties, that he will long shed bitter tears over his fault, and will never be consoled."[1]

---

[1] In writing this, Rousseau thought of his own sad example; see *Confessions*, Bk. XIII. At the same time, he was glad that the Duchess of Luxembourg, who tried to find his abandoned chil-

In spite of this, Rousseau, with singular inconsistency, shrinks from attempting to show in detail how parents may educate their own children. Instead of this, he selects circumstances altogether exceptional and artificial. "I have resolved to give myself an imaginary pupil, to suppose myself of the proper age, and possessed of health, knowledge, and all the talents required by one who would labor on his education, and to guide him from the moment of his birth to the moment when, as a full-grown man, he will require no guide but himself." The model tutor must be young, boyish in tastes and feeling, and above accepting money for his services. "There are professions so noble, that no one can pursue them for money without showing that he is unworthy to pursue them." He must be willing to take charge of his pupil for twenty-five years; for change of tutors is fatal. He must realize that he has but one duty, — to teach his pupil the duties of man. As to the pupil, he must be of good family, of robust health, of ordinary ability, rich,[1] born in a temperate climate, preferably in France, and — an orphan. The tutor will choose for his ward, at birth, a nurse healthy in body and in heart, of good character and temperate habits, cleanly, gentle, patient, and willing to remain with the child as long as it needs a nurse. The tutor and the nurse must be in complete accord, and the child never dream of any change of government; in short, the tutor will

dren, did not succeed. Rousseau's finest theories had nothing to do with his practice. He was moral only for rhetorical purposes, and in imagination.

[1] "The poor," he says, "need no education; that furnished by their condition is compulsory; they can have no other."

order everything. The directions which Rousseau gives regarding the treatment and food of the infant, and the regimen and mode of life of the nurse are, in the main, excellent. They may be summed up in the one precept: Let Nature have her way. "The child at birth is already the pupil, not of the tutor, but of Nature. The tutor merely studies under this first teacher and prevents her efforts from being balked. He watches the baby, observes it, follows it, descries the first dawning of its feeble intelligence."

Rousseau rightly insists that man's education begins at his birth, and that what is acquired unconsciously far exceeds, in amount and importance, what is acquired consciously and through instruction.[1] "All is instruction for animate, sensible beings." What he says with regard to the gradual growth of a world in the child's consciousness[2] is in every way admirable, and forestalls many of the results of our latest psychology. Rousseau, indeed, was a psychologist of the first rank. "The first sensations of children," he says, "are purely affective; they perceive only pleasure and pain. Being unable either to walk or grasp, they require a great deal of time for the gradual formation of those representative sensations[3] which show

---

[1] This is a truth to which kindergærtners ought to give serious heed.

[2] Had he pursued this thought, and not been led astray by his own personal feelings, he would have told us that education is nothing more or less than the formation, in the child's consciousness, of a rational world, that is, of a world in which every object and act has its true distinguishing relations for intellect, and its true distinguishing value for affection.

[3] Pre-Kantian metaphysics still allowed people to use such expressions as this; but in the next clause Rousseau shows that he has a glimpse of the truth.

them the objects outside of themselves; but, while these objects are multiplying, withdrawing, so to speak, from their eyes, and assuming for them dimensions and shapes, the return of the affective sensations begins to subject them to the rule of habit"; and habit is something to be avoided. "Food and sleep, too exactly measured, become necessary for them at stated intervals; and soon the desire arises, not from need, but from habit; or, rather, habit adds a new need to that of Nature. This must be prevented." . . . "The only habit which the child should be allowed to contract is the habit of contracting none. Let it not be carried on one arm more than on the other; let it not be accustomed to offer one hand rather than the other, or to use it more frequently, to eat, sleep, act at stated times, or to be unable to remain alone either night or day. Prepare, a long way in advance, for the dominion of its freedom, and the use of its powers, by leaving its body to its natural habits, and placing it in a condition to be always its own master, and in all things to carry out its own will, as soon as it has one."[1]

[1] These precepts are both unnatural and unwise. Even in a "state of Nature," children learn habits from the very first. Indeed, it may be safely said that all evolution, whether in Nature or Culture, is due to the acquisition of habits. Habit is merely the incarnation and organization of experience and action, by which both become easier and richer, and leave room for advance. It is economy of energy. To be consistent, Rousseau ought to have said: Do not allow the child to see with its eyes, rather than its ears, or to walk on its feet rather than on its head. Seeing with the eyes is no less the result of habit than right-handedness. And what is all excellence but perfected habit? How does the great musician learn to play or sing except by habit? What is all social life but an agreement about habits? What is language but the

What Rousseau next says of the necessity and the method of freeing the child early, by careful habituation (!), from those irrational fears and repulsions which derange so many lives — fear of spiders, toads, mice, masks, detonations, darkness, etc. — is excellent; but he records a very exceptional experience when he says, "I have never seen a peasant — man, woman, or child — afraid of spiders." Much of that unlovely trait of fastidiousness, which at the present day so often degenerates into cruel unsympathy for all that is not immaculate, sweet-scented, and æsthetic, is due to a neglect of Rousseau's precepts.

In course of time, the child emerges from mere "affective" sensations, and begins to construct, out of that portion of these which is less urgent, a world of things in time and space. What Rousseau has to say of this transition contains much truth, and testifies to fine observation; but it is marred throughout by a false metaphysics, which made him think that the world of external objects is one thing, and the system of his organized sensations another. What can we say to a passage like the following, for example? "In the early part of life, when memory and imagina-

habit of using the same sounds for the same thoughts? Had Rousseau said that, while education is the acquisition of habits that create a world of harmony between the individual and his fellow-beings, conscious and unconscious, and, therefore, the very condition of life and progress, yet the individual should be careful not to allow any habit to master him, when it proves prejudicial to such life or progress, he would have uttered a great and fruitful truth. But his whole vision was dimmed by the false notion that the normal man is the natural man, and the latter a solitary savage, obedient to his momentary instincts and caprices. Such a man never did, or could, exist

tion are still inactive, the child attends only to what affects its senses. Its sensations being the first materials of its knowledge, by offering them to it in a suitable order we are preparing its memory to furnish them, later, in the same order, to its understanding; but, since it attends only to its sensations, it is enough at first to show it very distinctly the connection of these same sensations with the objects that cause them." Just as if the very objects were not groups of sensations, already organized into things in time and space, by the activity of the distinguishing understanding! And as if a child, attentive only to sensations, could be conscious of any objects to refer them to! When it is conscious of such objects, its understanding has already been at work in complicated and far-reaching ways. Rousseau's prejudice in favor of sensation, and against understanding, closed his eyes to the most obvious facts, and led him into the gravest errors with regard to early education.[1] Man is a "rational animal" from the first moment of his existence. His first *conscious* feeling, however vague, implies an act of the understanding, which is busy organizing sensations long before it knows anything of an "external world." His very body is but organized sensation. Rousseau, however, failing to see this, but recognizing that the notions of good and evil are due to reason, maintains that, in its earliest years, the child is incapable of any moral education: if controlled at all, it must be controlled by simple

---

[1] In this connection should be read Rosmini's unfinished work, *The Ruling Principle of Method in Education*, translated by Mrs. William Grey. Boston: D. C. Heath & Co.

force. "Reason alone," he says, "acquaints us with good and evil. The conscience, which makes us love the one and hate the other, though independent of reason, cannot develop without it.[1] Before the age of reason, we do good and evil without knowing that we do, and there is no morality in our actions, although there sometimes is in the feeling about others' actions having relation to us. A child tries to upset everything he sees; he breaks or rends everything he can lay his hands upon; he grasps a bird as he would a stone, and chokes it without knowing what he is doing."

Rousseau is entirely right in maintaining that such actions imply no innate evil on the part of the child, being merely so many modes in which it gives effective expression to its undisciplined activity; nor is he wrong when he says that the child's desire to dominate others and make them act for it — a desire which readily degenerates into tyranny, impatience, badness — proceeds from the same source. To prevent such degenerations, he lays down four maxims, whose intent, he says, is "to give more real liberty and less authority (*empire*) to children, to allow them to do more for themselves, and exact less from others." The gist of them is, that the child should be helped, as far as necessary, to do whatever is really necessary for its physical well-being, and no farther; that no attention should be paid to its whims, opinions, or

[1] Here again we have both bad psychology and bad metaphysics. That which cannot develop without something else is surely not independent of that something; for a thing is not distinct from its development. And surely the love of good is not something irrational; nor is the mind a group of separate "faculties."

irrational desires. This would be unexceptionable, if the child's *spiritual* needs had been taken into account; but the omission is characteristic of Rousseau.

The first book of *Émile* closes with a number of disconnected precepts, such as, that a child should never be allowed to have anything because it cries for it; that it should not be weaned too soon; that it should not be fed on milk gruel; that it should not have heaps of gaudy and expensive toys; that it should be made to cut its teeth on soft objects; that it should be confined to a small vocabulary, but taught to articulate its words correctly from the first. Most of these are wise, and certainly "according to Nature!"

CHAPTER VI

ROUSSEAU'S EDUCATIONAL THEORIES

CHILDHOOD

(*Émile*, Bk. II.)

Despise but Reason and Science, man's supreme power; allow thyself but to be confirmed by the Spirit of Lies in works of glamor and enchantment, then I have thee already without condition. — (Mephistopheles in) *Faust*, Pt. I., lines 1498-1502 (Schröer).

With the advent of language, infancy closes, and childhood, in the narrower sense, begins. Tears and cries, having now found a substitute, should be discouraged, and every effort made to free the child from timidity and querulousness. Dangerous weapons and fire should be kept out of his way; but otherwise he should be allowed the utmost freedom, and as little notice as possible taken of his occasional bumps and bruises, which are valuable experiences. He should not be taught anything that he can naturally find out for himself — not even to walk or climb. Having complete freedom, he will get a few contusions, but therewith a great deal of invaluable training. "It is at this second stage," says Rousseau, "that the life of the individual properly begins; it is now that he attains self-consciousness. Memory extends the feeling of identity to all the moments of his existence;

he becomes truly one and the same, and consequently already capable of happiness or misery. He must henceforth be considered as a moral being." This is, indeed, a new stage!

To Rousseau, moral existence obviously means capability of happiness or misery. To be moral is to be happy; to be immoral is to be miserable; and, given his point of view, no other conclusion could well have been reached. It follows that every effort ought to be made to insure the happiness of the child. "Of children that are born," he says, "half, at most, reach adolescence, and your pupil will probably never reach manhood. What, then, are we to think of that barbarous education which sacrifices the present to an uncertain future, which loads a child with all sorts of chains, and begins by rendering it miserable, in order to prepare for it some distant, pretended happiness, which it will probably never enjoy?" . . . "Who knows how many children perish victims of the extravagant wisdom of a father or a teacher? Happy to escape from his cruelty, they derive no other advantage from the woes he has made them suffer than this, that they die without regretting a life of which they have known only the torments." . . . "Fathers, do you know the moment when death awaits your children? Do not prepare regret for yourselves by depriving them of the few moments which Nature lends them. As soon as they are able to feel the pleasure of being, see that they enjoy it; take care that, whenever it may please God to call them, they do not die without having tasted life." . . . "You will tell me that this is the time for correcting man's evil inclinations; that it is in childhood, when pains are least felt, that we should multiply them, in order to forestall them for the age of reason. But who has told you that this arrangement is within your power, or that all these fine instructions, with which you load the weak mind of a child, will not one day be more pernicious than useful to him?" . . . "Why do you impose on him more evils than his condition can bear, without being sure that these present evils will be made up for in the future? And how will you prove to me that those evil inclinations, which you pretend to cure, do not come from your ill-advised care, far more than from Nature? Miserable foresight, which renders a being unhappy in the present, in the ill-founded hope of making him happy in the future!" . . . "We do not know what absolute happiness or unhappiness is. Everything is mixed in this life. We never taste a pure feeling; we are never two minutes in the same state." . . . "Good and evil are common to us all, but in different degrees. The happiest is he who suffers fewest pains; the unhappiest he who feels fewest pleasures. Always there are more sufferings than enjoyments: that is the difference common to all. The felicity of man here below is, therefore, only a negative state. It must be estimated by the smallness of the number of evils which he suffers."

"Every feeling of pain is inseparable from the desire to be delivered from it; every idea of pleasure is inseparable from the desire to enjoy it; every desire supposes privation. Hence, it is in the disproportion between our desires and our faculties that our misery lies." . . . "Where, then, lies human wisdom or the way to true happiness?" . . . "It lies in diminishing the excess of our desires over our faculties, and establishing a perfect equality between power and will. It is only when this is done that, though all the powers are in action, the soul will, nevertheless, remain peaceful, and man be well ordered. It is thus that Nature, which does everything for the best, arranged matters at the beginning." . . . "It is only in this primitive state that equilibrium between power and desire is found, and that man is not unhappy." . . . "It is the imagination that extends for us the measure of things possible, whether in good or evil, and which, consequently, excites and nourishes the desires with the hope of satisfaction. But the object, which at first seemed close at hand, flees quicker than we can pursue it. When we think we are reaching it, it transforms itself and appears afar off." . . . "Thus we exhaust ourselves, without reaching our goal, and the more we gain on enjoyment, the further happiness withdraws from us. On the other hand, the nearer man remains to his natural condition, the smaller is the difference between his faculties and his desires, and, therefore, the less distance is he removed from happiness. He is never less miserable than when he seems deprived of all;[1] for misery does not consist in being deprived of things, but in the need which is felt for them." . . . "The real world has its limits; the world of the imagination is infinite. Being unable to enlarge the one, let us contract the

[1] It is Rousseau the vagabond that speaks here. See pages 33 sq.

other." ... "When we say that man is weak, what do we mean? The word weakness signifies a relation." ... "He whose power is greater than his needs, were he an insect or a worm, is a strong being. He whose needs are greater than his power, were he a conqueror, a hero, or a god, is a weak being. Man is very strong when he is content to be what he is; he is very weak when he tries to rise above humanity.[1] Do not, therefore, imagine that, in enlarging your faculties, you are enlarging your powers. On the contrary, you are diminishing them, if your pride enlarges more yet." ... "It is by laboring to increase our happiness that we turn it into misery. Any man who should be contented to live merely, would live happy, and therefore would live good; for what advantage would he have in being bad?"

"Everything is folly and contradiction in human institutions." ... "Foresight! foresight, which continually carries us beyond ourselves, and often places us where we shall never really arrive, is the true source of all our miseries. What folly for an ephemeral being, like man, to be looking forever into a distant future, which rarely comes, and to neglect the present, of which he is sure!" ... "Is it Nature that thus carries men so far from themselves?" ... "O man! concentrate thine existence within thyself, and thou wilt no longer be miserable. Remain in the place which Nature has assigned thee in the scale of beings; nothing can make thee leave it. Do not recalcitrate against the hard law of necessity,

[1] Gœthe, *Faust*, Prologue in Heaven, puts this sentiment in th mouth of Mephistopheles. Lines 45–50, 58–65.

and do not, by trying to resist it, exhaust the powers which heaven has lent thee, not to extend or prolong thine existence, but merely to preserve it, as, and as long as, it pleases the same. Thy liberty, thy power, extend only as far as thy natural forces, and no further. All the rest is but slavery, illusion, prestige." . . . "Even dominion is servile, when it rests on opinion; for thou dependest on the prejudices of those thou governest through prejudice." . . . "The only man who does his will is he who, in order to do so, has no need to eke out his own arms with those of another; whence it follows that *the first of all blessings is not authority, but liberty. This is my fundamental maxim.* We have but to apply it to childhood, and all the rules of education will flow from it."

It has seemed well to make this long quotation, because it contains Rousseau's fundamental view of life, and the kernel of his educational theory. The end of life is happiness, and happiness is the sensuous enjoyment of each moment, as it passes, without thought, plan, or aspiration for higher things, nay, without regard to others. All efforts after a divine life of deep insight, strong, just affection, and far-reaching beneficent will; all unions among men for the realization of this life, in and through society, are folly and contradiction. To live as the beast lives, in his appointed place, is the chief end of man. Because some children die before they reach youth or manhood, it is cruel to deprive any, through discipline, self-denying, continuous tasks, or thought of the future, of the manifold, thoughtless delights of the present. Discipline and self-control have no value in themselves; at best they are but means for future pleasure. The child that dies without having enjoyed pleasure has not "tasted of life." No matter what his spiritual attainments, or the beauty and nobility of his character, his existence has been a failure. Whatever interferes with present pleasure is evil.

It would hardly be possible to form a more pitiful conception of human life and education than this. There is not a moral or noble trait in it. The truth is, Rousseau was so purely a creature of sense and undisciplined impulse that he never, for one moment, rose to a consciousness of any moral life at all. He could not, therefore, take delight in it. *Noblesse oblige*, the ruling maxim of the unselfish, moral, and social man, was in him replaced by the maxim of the selfish, undutiful churl and reprobate, *Bonheur invite*. But, in spite of all this, nay, by reason of it, Rousseau and his theories are most interesting and fruitful objects of study. In days when uncontrolled individualism still has its advocates, it is well fully to realize what it means. And this is what Rousseau has told us, in a siren song of mock-prophetic unction, which readily captivates and lures to destruction vast crowds of thoughtless sentimentalists. He has told us, further, in the same tone, how children may be prepared for a life of individualism; and his sense-drunk ravings, in denunciation of all moral discipline, have been, and still are, received as divine oracles by millions of parents and teachers, who have the training of children in their hands. And hence it has come to pass that the old maxim: Train up a child in the way that he should go, has been replaced by this other:

See that the child have a "good time." No wonder that Good Time has become the chief American god!

Rousseau's education according to Nature, starting from an utterly calumnious notion of child-nature, and of human nature in general, and ignoring all that is characteristic and noble in both, proves to be an education for pure, reckless individualism, destructive of all social institutions, and all true civilization. Its aim is the undisputed rule of caprice.

But to proceed. True to his principles, Rousseau maintains that children should not be taught obedience:[1] their relations to persons should be exactly the same as their relations to things, which resist, but do not command. Human relations should be replaced by mechanical relations, if the precious individuality of the child is to be safeguarded. When a child tries to go beyond his natural limitations, he is not to be forbidden, but prevented. He is to meet the iron law of Nature everywhere, the love of humanity nowhere. Nature is to be all in all.

If children are not to obey, neither are they to command — not even when they accompany their commands with *Please*, or *If you please*. They are to be listened to only when they ask for things good for them. "The surest way to render your child miserable is to accustom him to obtain everything he wants." His needs are really few, and the fewer the better. By humoring him, you make him a despot,

---

[1] "No one," he says, "not even the father, has a right to command a child to do what is of no good to him." Were he commanded to do what is good for others, he might in time become generous, and degenerate into civilization. Cf. Carpenter's *Civilization, its Cause and Cure*.

"at once the vilest of slaves and the wretchedest of creatures." . . . "Weakness, united with despotism, begets but folly and misery." The rule is: "Give to children, as far as possible, everything that can afford them a real pleasure; refuse them whatever they ask from a mere whim, or to perform an act of authority."

Of course, children, as natural creatures, are never to be reasoned with: Nature never reasons. "I see nothing more stupid," says Rousseau, "than children that have been reasoned with." . . . "Use force with children, and reason with men; such is the natural order." Moreover, such things as loyalty to parents, and affectionate respect for their wishes, as such, must never be appealed to. The result might be deference, something altogether unknown to Nature and hostile to liberty. The child must be guided solely by the hard yoke of natural necessity. "Thus you will render him patient, equable, resigned, and peaceful, even when he does not get what he wishes; for it is in the nature of man to endure patiently the necessity of things, but not the ill will of others." . . . "No one ought to undertake to rear a child, unless he knows how to guide him where he wishes by the sole laws of the possible and the impossible. The sphere of both being equally unknown to him, may be widened or narrowed about him as one pleases. He may be bound, pushed, or held back, with merely the chain of necessity, without his murmuring. He may be rendered supple and docile by the mere force of things, and vice have no occasion to spring up in him; for the passions are never roused so long as they are without effect." In this way he will never learn what kindness is, and so acquire the unnatural sentiment of gratitude, or, indeed, any sentiment of a human sort. He will be as natural as a kitten!

It follows from such principles that the child must neither be chidden, punished, nor called upon to beg pardon. "Devoid of all morality in his actions, he can do nothing that is morally evil, or that deserves chastisement or reprimand." And yet the child was declared, a little before, to be a moral being (see p. 114).

Returning once more to his favorite incontestable maxim, "that the first movements of Nature are always right: that there is no original perversity in the human heart," Rousseau insists that "the greatest, most important, and most useful rule of all education is, not to gain time, but to lose it." . . . "Early education must, therefore, be purely negative. It consists, not in teaching virtue or truth, but in guarding the heart from vice and the mind from error. If you could do nothing, and allow nothing to be done; if you could guide your pupil, healthy and robust, to the age of twelve years, without his being able to distinguish his right hand from his left, — the eyes of his understanding would open to reason at your first lessons. Without prejudices, without habits, he would have nothing to counteract the effect of your solicitude. He would soon become in your hands the wisest of men; and, by beginning with doing nothing, you would have made a prodigy of education." . . . "Do the opposite of what is usually done, and you will always do well." . . . "Exercise the child's body, his organs, his senses, his strength; but keep his mind indolent as long as possible." . . . "Look upon all delays as advantages . . . let childhood ripen in children." . . . "If a lesson has to be given, do not give it to-day, if it can be put off till to-morrow."

This is what Rousseau calls natural education; but it is, in fact, almost the most artificial education conceivable. It is cloistral and worse. Nature is made to exclude its highest manifestations, and then the child, instead of being allowed to come freely in contact with the brute remainder, is watched, dogged, guided, and forcibly controlled at every step; and all for the sake of keeping him in a condition of submoral, sub-human innocence. Rousseau forgot that a child's capacity for enjoyment even is proportioned to his intelligence; and so, while he maintained that a child should not be deprived of present, for the sake of future, pleasure, for fear that the latter might never come, he insisted that he should be deprived of present, for the sake of future, instruction, though the latter is subject to the same risks. But Rousseau thought of his own early corruption, and despised logic. We have only to compare the twelve-year-old American boy, who, mixing freely with Nature, in its broadest sense, contrives, by pluck, intelligence, and cloisterless self-control, to earn his own, and perhaps others', livelihood, with Rousseau's helpless, artificial product, to realize the value of his educational system.

"But where," says Rousseau, "shall we place this child, in order to rear him thus, *like an insensible being, an automaton?* Shall we keep him in the moon? Or in a desert island? Shall we remove him from human kind? Will he not have continually before him, in the world, the spectacle and example of others' passions? Will he never see other children of his own age? Will he not see his relations, nurse, governess, footman, and even his tutor, who, after all, will not be an angel?" Rousseau feels the difficulty of these questions, and answers that the tutor must do his best to be an angel, and then retire, with his pupil, to a remote country village, where, by inspiring the villagers with respect and affection, he can practically control everybody and everything, and be beyond reach of the evil influence of cities. In this retreat, the child, entirely in the hands of his unpaid tutor, and dependent on his resources for everything, will vegetate, and learn what he cannot help, by examples. When he sees a peasant angry, he will be told that he is ill, and thus learn to avoid anger. When he plants beans in a peasant's melon-patch, and, after he has spent much care on them, the peasant comes and pulls them up, "the heart-broken child will fill the air with sobs and screams,"[1] and have his first feeling of injustice.[2] On learning, however, that the peasant has only done to him what he has first done to the peasant, and that, besides, the land belongs to the peasant, he will come to have a feeling of justice. One of the tutor's chief duties will be to arrange for practical lessons of this sort. If the pupil breaks a pane of glass in his room, the tutor will say

---

[1] Is this one of the results of "peaceful" Nature-education?

[2] This is incorrect. He would feel merely disappointment, not even resentment. The catastrophe might be due to "Nature," for aught he knew. There are no *feelings* of justice and injustice.

nothing, but leave it unrepaired until the pupil catches a violent cold,[1] and then have it replaced. If he breaks it a second time, the tutor will remove him to a dark room, and shut him up there, until he voluntarily agrees to break no more panes. How this differs from punishment, it is not easy to see.[2] Rousseau evidently thinks that moral feelings can be roused in a child by bringing home to him the consequences of his deeds. There is no greater mistake in the world.[3] A child may learn selfish prudence in this way; but the morality of acts has nothing to do with their *actual* consequences, but only with their *intended* consequences. An immoral act does not become moral, because it brings desirable consequences. Even brute beasts learn prudence by Rousseau's moral method; but they never rise to morality. All the morality there is connected with an act is realized, as a personal quality, before the performance of the act.

With the rise of the moral consciousness comes the possibility of evil, and, among other things, of lying, with a view to escape consequences. Rousseau justly distinguishes two kinds of lies: (1) intentional misstatements of facts; (2) promises not intended to be kept; and he has some sensible remarks about what lying means to young children; but, when he tells us that "trying to teach them to tell the truth is simply teaching them to lie," those who have had experience

---

[1] This result is purely arbitrary, depending not only on the season, but upon the position of the child's bed.

[2] In any case, he is not being educated by Nature.

[3] Herbert Spencer's work on education is vitiated throughout by this error.

with children can only express utter disagreement with him. Again, when he tells us that the true way to cure a child of lying is to make him see that it is not his interest to lie, we can only say that he is propounding a most immoral and pernicious doctrine — albeit it is of a piece with his whole ethical teaching. A child that tells the truth only when he thinks it profitable so to do, will tell lies under the same circumstances. Lying is simply one manifestation of cowardice, or feebleness of will, as against undifferentiated instinct, and can be cured only by a process which strengthens the will, by the development of intelligence, and the subjection of instinct. But Rousseau's whole system is intended to enable men to dispense with the need of willing, by arranging things so that they shall always be able to follow their instincts — as he did!

Generosity, meaning almsgiving, is to be taught in this way: "Instead of being in haste to exact acts of charity from my pupil, I prefer to perform them in his presence, and to deprive him of the means of imitating me in that, as an honor that does not belong to his age." . . . "If, seeing me assist the poor, he questions me about it, and it is the proper time to reply, I shall say to him: 'My friend, when the poor agreed that there should be rich people, the rich promised to maintain all those who should not have the means of living, either from their property, or their labor.'[1] 'And you also have promised that?' he will ask. 'Of course (I will say); I am master of the wealth that passes through my hands, only on the

[1] This is, of course, a pious lie.

condition attached to owning it.' After hearing these words . . . another than Émile would be tempted to imitate me, and play the rich man; in such case, I should at least prevent him from doing so with ostentation. I should prefer to have him usurp my right, and give surreptitiously. This is a fraud natural to his age, and the only one I should forgive in him." In other words, Émile would not give at all, or give through vanity, as a rich man!

Rousseau admits that all virtues acquired in this way are merely monkey virtues, unreflective imitations, and therefore not moral; and, though fully conscious of the possible evils springing from imitation, he yet insists that no other virtues are possible for the child. In this, he modestly makes his own nature the measure of possibility for the race.

The only moral lesson that he would teach children is "to do harm to nobody. The injunction to do good, unless subordinate to this, is dangerous, false, and contradictory. Who is there that does no good? The wicked man does good, like other people; he makes one happy by making a hundred unhappy; and hence come all our calamities. The loftiest virtues are negative; they are also the most difficult, because they are without show, and above the pleasure, so dear to the heart of man, of knowing that some one else is pleased with us." This is, of course, the purest sophistry — as if doing good to one, at the expense of a hundred, were doing good at all! The precept, Do good, includes the precept, Do no evil. But Rousseau always wanted a plea for doing nothing, and he was not above resorting to the most pitiful sophistry in order to obtain one — as, for instance, in his attempt to justify himself for turning his children over to the foundling hospital.[1] The fact here referred to must be allowed to have its full weight in our estimate of Rousseau's educational theories. It shows (1) that he had no natural love for children, and no interest in them — except, of course, a picturesque one: they were touching features in a landscape; (2) that, while devoted to sensuality, he had no sense of even the most sacred of duties. Hence his attempt to show that the most sublime virtues are negative — a most comfortable doctrine, amounting to this: Do nothing, and you will do sublimely well. From this maxim Rousseau drew the following conclusion, whose bearing is but too obvious: "The injunction never to injure others, involves the injunction to have as little to do with society as possible; for in the social state, the good of one is necessarily the evil of another. This relation being in the essence of the thing, nothing can alter it."[2]

It is impossible here to enumerate all the educational precepts that Rousseau, from this point of view, lays down; but they may be summed up under three general heads: (1) Do everything to place children in easy, fearless contact with sub-human nature and its

[1] *Confessions*, Bks. VII., VIII.

[2] Then follows the second quotation at the head of Chapter V. It is needless to say that the assertion itself is the exact opposite of the truth, and subversive of all civilization. Cf. Lowell's fine line in *The Present Crisis:*

"In the gain or loss of one race, all the rest have equal claim,"

and Creon's first speech in Sophocles' *Antigone*.

necessary laws; that is, make them, as far as possible, automata;[1] (2) Do everything to prevent their having any relations to human nature, as such, by withdrawing them, as far as possible, from society, and turning those persons with whom they *must* come in contact into automata; (3) Hoodwink them into thinking that everything which you, as the representative of Nature, desire them to do, is imposed by natural necessity.[2]

In accordance with the first of these, children are to have their muscles, nerves, and senses carefully trained, in savage fashion. They are to be encouraged, or bribed,[3] to run, leap, climb, balance themselves, and to move heavy masses. They are to

---

[1] Cf. quotation on p. 123.

[2] "Are not all his surroundings, as far as they relate to him, under your control?" . . . "Of course, he must do only what he wishes; but he must wish only what you wish him to do. He must take no step that you have not foreseen, nor open his mouth without your knowing beforehand what he is going to say." — *Émile*, Bk. II. Such is Education according to Nature! Rousseau's long intimacy with the Jesuits had not been for nothing. Their cadaver is Rousseau's automaton; and his methods match theirs. Grimm said of him: "I know but one man who might have written an apology for the Jesuits in fine style . . . and that man is M. Rousseau." After all, a God-animated corpse is better than an automaton. But neither has any moral freedom.

[3] Chiefly with cakes and candy, of which Rousseau himself was very fond. "The proper way to govern children," he says, "is to guide them by the mouth. Gluttony, as a motive, is, of all things, preferable to vanity, because the former is a natural appetite, directly connected with the senses, whereas the latter is the product of opinion, subject to human caprice and all sorts of abuses." This is, of course, untrue. Darwin has shown that vanity is a common passion even among the lower animals, while Rousseau himself maintains that the animals are never gluttonous, — which again is untrue!

swim,[1] to go about bareheaded and barefooted, in light, loose, gay clothing; to sleep on a hard bed; to be waked up at any hour; to be inured to heat, cold, knocks, and bruises; to eat when they are hungry, and drink when they are thirsty — cold water, even when they are in a flood of perspiration. They are to play nightly games, involving lonely visits to forests, churches, and graveyards; they are to walk, and to find things, in the dark, without fear or hesitation.[2] They are not to be vaccinated, because vaccination, though bringing certain advantages, requires the services of a physician — which must be avoided like poison.[3] Riding is not favored, because it is an exercise not within the reach of everybody. Besides, Rousseau himself disliked it. The different senses are to be carefully cultivated. "To exercise the senses is not merely to make use of them, but to learn to judge by means of them, to learn, so to speak, to feel; for we can neither touch, see, nor hear, except as we have learnt." In exercising the sense of touch, the nocturnal games, above referred to, are especially valuable; they may even enable us

---

[1] "Émile will be as much at home in the water as on land. Why cannot he live in all the elements? If he could be taught to fly in the air, I should make him an eagle; I should make him a salamander, if he could be inured to fire."

[2] They are to be tempted to this, as usual, with candy! In this way, their *natural* dread of the dark is to be overcome. And yet we are told that "the caprice of children is never the work of Nature, but of bad discipline: they have either obeyed or commanded."

[3] "If we give a child small-pox, we shall have the advantage of foreseeing and foreknowing his disease; but if he takes it naturally, we shall have saved him from the doctor, which is a still greater advantage."

to dispense with the senses of sight and hearing — apparently a great advantage.[1] The use of keyless stringed instruments dulls the sense of touch. The ideal instrument is the piano — which Rousseau himself played! Numerous instructions are given as to how the eye is to be trained to estimate weights, distances, etc. Some of the exercises are delightfully complicated, involving the inevitable candy, which, though rather a civilized product, seems to be Nature's bribe. This is the place for drawing and painting; but the objects selected must always be in Nature, never copies or casts.[2] In connection with all this, Rousseau has some admirable observations upon the way in which the notion of space is acquired, although there is a sad want of close thinking displayed in the delightful remark that "the whole universe can be only a point for an oyster." It would not even be a point; for a point is a very complicated conception,

[1] "We are blind half our lives, with this difference, that those who are really blind can always guide themselves, while we do not venture to take a step into the heart of the night. There are lanterns, I shall be told. Yes, yes! always machines! Who can assure you that they will follow you everywhere when you want them? I prefer that Émile should have eyes in the ends of his fingers rather than in the chandler's shop." . . . "By putting one hand upon the body of a violoncello, one may, without the help of eyes or ears, distinguish, by the mere vibration or quivering of the wood, whether the sound produced is high or low." . . . "If we would exercise our senses on these differences, I have no doubt that in time one might feel a whole tune with his fingers. If this be admitted, it follows that we might speak to the deaf in music." But alas! the violoncello is a machine, M. Rousseau!

[2] Émile's room is to be adorned with his own drawings and paintings, placed in more and more elaborate frames in proportion to their badness. Thus the expression, "fit for a gilt frame," is to suggest a moral lesson, valuable later on.

involving the consciousness of space. For cultivating the sense of form, practical geometry, a matter of strings and cut paper, is recommended. Reasoned geometry is, of course, forbidden.

For training the sense of hearing there are various means, chief among which is music. This, being a favorite occupation with Rousseau, is allowed the use of civilized instruments. Taste, with which smell is closely connected, is to be cultivated by the use of simple, natural food. "The Supreme Goodness, which has made the pleasure of sensible beings the instrument of their preservation, shows us, by what pleases our palates, what is suitable for our stomachs. When Nature is allowed her way, there is no safer physician for a man than his own appetite. In his primitive state, I have no doubt that the foods which he found most pleasant were also the most wholesome." Gluttony, being natural, is excused in this way. "Since the whole of childhood is, or ought to be, merely a succession of games and gleesome amusements, I do not see why pure bodily exercises should not have a material and sensible prize." On the same principle, mental exercises ought to be rewarded with an abstract triangle, a fair Platonic idea, or a pleasant aspect of transcendental being! But of such exercises he does not approve. Singularly enough, Rousseau, who professes to give directions for rearing children in a state of Nature, maintains that they should not be allowed to touch animal food, which, if not bad for health, is bad for character. "It is certain that great meat-eaters are, generally, more cruel and fierce than other men." . . . "The bar-

barity of the English is well known, whereas the Gaures are the gentlest of men. All savages are cruel, and this is not due to their character, but to their food." This is one of those delicious inconsistencies of which Rousseau is full. The truth is that, for him, savage and Jean Jacques meant the same thing, and of that thing he has a very good opinion. He says, elsewhere, that savages, "known for their keen sensibility, are still more so for their subtlety of mind." But the gentle savage, Jean Jacques, did not like meat, and so that must be a perversion of savagery. His assertion, moreover, that the savage, "having no prescribed task, obeying no law but his own will, is forced to reason at every action of his life," only shows that he knew nothing of real savage life.

In pursuance of the second maxim, children are to receive no instruction that would carry them beyond the range of their own actual sense-experience, or even to reason to the conditions of that experience. Every kind of instruction drawing upon the past or present experience of the race — History, Geography, Grammar, Languages, Literature (even La Fontaine's Fables), Science — is to be excluded. There is to be no learning by heart, no declamation, no examination, no verbal expression of knowledge. "Émile will not chatter, he will act." All efforts at cleverness and bright remarks, all talkativeness, must be frowned down. Books are to be tabooed. "By removing all the duties of children," says Rousseau, "I remove the instruments of their greatest misery, namely, books. Reading is curse of childhood,[1] and almost the only

[1] This is not true; but Rousseau read bad books.

occupation that people can invent for it. At twelve years of age, Émile will hardly know what a book is. But, I shall be told, he must at least know how to read, when reading is useful to him." . . . "If we must demand nothing of children through obedience, it follows that they can learn nothing of which they do not feel the actual present advantage, in the form either of pleasure or of use: otherwise, what motive should prompt them to learn it? The art of talking and listening to absent friends . . . is an art that can be rendered sensible to human beings at any age. By what miracle has this useful and pleasant art become a torment to children? Because we force them to apply themselves to it against their wills, and put it to uses of which they understand nothing. A child is never very eager to perfect the instrument with which he is tortured. But make this instrument minister to his pleasures, and he will soon apply himself to it in spite of you." . . . "The present interest is the great motive, and the only one that leads safely and far. Émile sometimes receives from his father, mother, relatives, friends,[1] notes of invitation for a dinner, a walk, a boating-party, a public festival. These notes are short, clear, neat, and well written. Some one must be found to read them. This some one is not found at the right moment, or pays the child out for some disobliging conduct of the day before. Thus the opportunity, the moment, passes. The note is at last read to him; but it is too late! Oh! if he had only been able to read himself!

[1] N.B. Émile is supposed to be an orphan, and to live apart from society.

Others are received: they are so short; the subject of them is so interesting; he would like to decipher them; sometimes he finds help and sometimes a refusal. He exerts himself and finally deciphers half of a note: it is an invitation to go to-morrow to eat cream — he does not know where or with whom. How he struggles to read the rest!" . . . "Shall I speak now of writing? No; I am ashamed to amuse myself with such nonsense in a treatise on education." This is a typical specimen of Rousseau's natural method, which, assuming that the child has only animal motives, makes no effort to correct or replace them. What notion of man and society would be suggested to a child, if the people about him, in order to be even with him, — poor little animal! — should refuse to read a note for him? It is safe to say that it would be both hateful and false, — in fact, Rousseau's own diseased notion (see p. 74). For Rousseau hated the human in humanity: he hated science,[1] true love, and energy of will, being incapable of all

[1] He says: "I teach my pupil a very long and very painful art — the art of being ignorant; for the science of any one who does not flatter himself that he knows more than he really does know, reduces itself to very small bulk." The martyrdom of study is described in these affecting terms: "The clock strikes. What a change! In an instant, his eye loses its lustre; his gayety vanishes. Good-bye to joy! good-bye to gleesome games! A severe, ill-tempered man takes him by the hand, and gravely says to him: 'Let us go, sir,' and leads him away. In the room which they enter, I catch a glimpse of books. Books! what sad furniture for his age! The poor child submits to being dragged along, turns a regretful eye upon everything about him, holds his peace, and goes off, his eyes swollen with tears which he dare not shed, and his heart big with sighs which he dare not give vent to." It is needless to comment on such stuff!

three. Hence he deprecated all culture of intellect, affection, and will, of all that makes man, life, and the world human.

Of the third maxim it is sufficient to say that, according to Rousseau, children are to be so managed that what is, in reality, the result of the most careful forethought, shall seem natural and necessary; in other words, that they shall, from first to last, be victims of a pious fraud. By means of this, the child is to be dehumanized, to be made a victim and a dupe. How small must his intelligence and his observation be, to make such dupery possible!

CHAPTER VII

ROUSSEAU'S EDUCATIONAL THEORIES

BOYHOOD

(*Émile*, Bk. III.)

I slept and dreamt that life was Beauty:
I woke and found that life was Duty.

When a boy has learnt his letters and is beginning to understand what is written, as before he understood only what was spoken, they put into his hands the works of great poets, which he reads at school; in these are contained . . . the encomia of ancient famous men, which he is required to learn by heart, in order that . . . he may desire to become like them.

PLATO, *Protagoras*.

ROUSSEAU's solitary pupil reaches the age of twelve years without having learnt to do anything but play. In playing, he has exercised his muscles, nerves, and senses. He has no knowledge of man; he does not reason; his sole motive is sensuous pleasure. But he is supple, alert, healthy, and docile, like a well-trained young dog. Moreover, he is exuberantly happy, because his strength is far in advance of his needs, and because the absorbing passion of manhood has not yet awakened in him. Thus the years from twelve to fifteen form a period of altogether exceptional free energy, which must be seized upon and directed — surreptitiously, of course — to the best ends, as Rousseau conceives them. This, in fact, is the time to cultivate the "sixth sense, which is called common sense, not so much because it is common to all men, as because it results from the well-regulated use of the other senses, and because it instructs us in the nature of things, through the convergence of all their appearances." "This sense," he continues, "has no special organ. It resides solely in the brain; and its sensations, which are purely internal, are called perceptions or ideas. It is by the number of these ideas that the extent of our knowledge is measured; it is their definiteness and clearness that constitutes correctness of thinking; it is the art of comparing them that we call human reason. Thus, what I called sensitive, or childish, reason consists in forming simple ideas, by the union of several sensations; and what I call intellectual or human reason consists in forming complex ideas, by the union of several simple ideas." It is hardly worth while to comment upon this crude, sensuous, chemical psychology. To have been condemned to it was the penalty paid by Rousseau for his superficial acquaintance with philosophy, and his contempt for it.

At this stage in their career, boys are still to be guided by immediate, sensuous interests. Moral motives are to play no part. The subjects suitable for study are few. Of the departments of knowledge within our reach, some are false, others useless, others only minister to the conceit of their possessors. The few that really contribute to our well-being are alone worthy of the attention of a wise man, and therefore of a child whom we mean to turn into one. Of these few, again, those must be excluded which demand for their study a developed intelligence, such, for example, as those dealing with the relations of man to man. What remains is the experimental natural sciences, whose objects are the visible heaven and earth. Curiosity now supervenes upon bodily restlessness, as a motive. But this curiosity is no mere mental or spiritual need of man's. "The innate desire for wellbeing, and the impossibility of completely satisfying it, make him continually seek for new means of contributing to it. Such is the first principle of curiosity, a principle natural to the human heart (!), but one whose development strictly keeps pace with our passions and our lights.[1] Banish a philosopher to a desert island, with instruments and books, and convince him that he must pass the remainder of his life there: he will hardly trouble himself any more about the system of the world, the laws of attraction, or the differential calculus. He will perhaps not open a book again in his life." This experiment, whose result is, to say the least, very doubtful, suffices to prove to Rousseau that these studies are not natural to man: therefore, they are to be ruled out.

"The island of the human race is the earth. The object that most strikes our eyes is the sun. As soon as we turn away from ourselves, our attention must direct itself to one or the other." Geography and astronomy are therefore now in order. But these subjects are not to be taught by means of books, maps,

[1] It never seems to have dawned for an instant upon Rousseau either that there could be any intellectual needs or motives, or that there was any value in a developed intelligence, as such.

globes, or charts. They are to be studied in the presence of the objects themselves, and that, too, in the most matter-of-fact fashion. No feeling in the presence of Nature's sublimities is to be looked for. "The child perceives objects; but he cannot perceive their relations; he cannot hear the sweet harmony of their concert." . . . "How shall the song of birds cause him a voluptuous emotion, if the accents of love and pleasure are still unknown to him?"

Rousseau reports various tricks and devices for inducing children to think what is implied in such natural phenomena as sunrise and sunset, and to represent it to themselves by means of circles and teetotums. The matter of geographical study is to be the country where the child lives, and the features of this he is to draw as well as he can. He is to be initiated into the mysteries of magnetism by means of wax ducks, modelled about a magnetic needle and made to swim about after a magnet. But lest he should plume himself upon this new and strange discovery, and take to showing it off, an elaborate conspiracy is entered into with a professional magician to humble his vanity, by trickery, in presence of an assembled and gaping crowd; and the poor child, guilty of having shown one natural feeling, is once more reduced to the condition of a marionette. Rousseau congratulates himself on the result. "All the detail of this example means more than it seems. How many lessons in one! How many mortifying consequences flow from the first movement of vanity! Young teacher, carefully watch this first movement! If you can make it produce humiliation and disgrace in this way, be sure it will be long before a second occurs. What elaborate preparations! you will say. I agree — and all to make a compass to take the place of a meridian."[1] This conspiracy is typical. In all cases the main thing is, not to impart knowledge to the child, but to guard him against the formation of false ideas, or the acceptance of any that do not grow out of his own individual experience. A secret effort may be made to secure his continuous attention; but constraint must never be applied. "It must always be pleasure or desire that produces this attention." . . . "It is always of less importance that the child should learn than that he should do nothing against his inclination." All attempts to make the child overcome his inclinations, in favor of moral action, are to be avoided, as useless and denaturalizing.

In course of time — toward the age of fifteen! — the child will begin to grow self-conscious, to know what is good for him, and to seek it. His good is simply sensuous well-being, without moral regard. He must now be induced to direct his mind to "useful objects," and the notion of the useful must now become his guiding star. He is to study nothing which he does not see to be useful for his own special sensuous ends. These are to be the limits of his curiosity. In fact, he is to be carefully trained in sordid selfishness, lest he should form false conceptions![2] If a child trained in this way should express doubts regarding the usefulness of astronomy to him, he is to be cured of them

[1] Quintilian was wiser when he said: "Vanity is a vice; but it is the parent of many virtues." See my *Aristotle*, p. 220.
[2] Compare the saying of Aristotle in my *Aristotle*, p. 189.

in this way. He and his tutor are to lose themselves in the forest. "We no longer," says Rousseau, "know where we are,[1] and when the time comes to return, we cannot find our way. The time passes; the heat comes; we are hungry; we hasten; we wander vainly from side to side." . . . "Much heated, much disappointed, very hungry, we only lose ourselves more and more. Finally, we sit down, not to rest, but to deliberate." . . . "After a few moments of silence, I say to him, in an anxious tone, 'My dear Émile, how are we to get out of this?'" Émile, "dripping with perspiration, and weeping bitter tears," replies, "'I know nothing about it. I'm tired; I'm hungry; I'm thirsty; I'm all used up.'" They finally look at their watches (Émile carries a watch!) and find that it is noon. Knowing that their home is to the south of the forest, and remembering that at noon the sun casts his shadow to the north, they thus find out the direction of the south, and, following it, are soon in sight of home. Hereupon Émile shouts: "Let us breakfast! let us dine! let us run quick! Astronomy is good for something." Thus he learns that astronomy is a useful science — useful in helping a big, tired, hungry cry-baby, accompanied by his tutor, to find his way home. And this is the child who has been reared as a savage, and taught to bear heat, cold, hunger, pain, fatigue, and to find his way in the dark!

"I hate books," says Rousseau; "they only teach us to talk about what we don't know." Nevertheless, Émile is, at last, to learn to read. Then his one book

[1] This, of course, is false as regards the tutor.

is to be — *Robinson Crusoe;* and the reason is this: "Robinson Crusoe, alone on his island, deprived of the aid of his fellow-men and of the instruments of all the arts, and, nevertheless, providing for his own subsistence and protection, and even attaining a certain sort of well-being, is an interesting object for any age, and may be rendered attractive to children in a thousand ways." . . . "This state, I admit, is not that of the social man . . . but it is by this same state that he must value all the rest. The surest way to rise above prejudice, and to shape one's judgment by the true relations of things, is to put oneself in the place of the isolated man, and to judge all things as this man, having regard to his own usefulness, must judge them." Émile will be fascinated with *Robinson Crusoe.* "I want him," says Rousseau, "to lose his head over it, to be continually absorbed by his castle, his goats, his plantations; to learn in detail, not by books, but by things, all that it is necessary to know in such a case; to imagine that he is Robinson himself, dressed in skins, wearing a big hat, a great sabre, and all the grotesque trappings of the figure, except the parasol, which he will not need. I wish him to be anxious about what he would do, if this or that should happen to fail, to examine his hero's conduct, to see if he has omitted anything, or if anything could be done better, to note carefully his faults, and to profit by them, so as not to commit similar ones; for you may be sure that he will plan to go and set up a similar establishment. This is the real air-castle of this blessed age, when one knows no other happiness than necessities and freedom." With these childish [1] thoughts in his head, he will be eager to learn all the "natural arts," that is, such arts as are necessary for the solitary man. He must, as long as possible, be prevented from taking any interest in those that require coöperation. "You see," says Rousseau, "thus far I have not spoken to my pupil about men. He would have too much good sense to listen to me. His relations with his kind are not yet pronounced enough to enable him to judge of others by himself. He knows no human being but himself, and himself very imperfectly; but, if he pronounces few judgments on himself, those he does pronounce are, at least, just. He knows nothing about the place of others; but he feels his own, and keeps himself in it. Instead of social laws, which he cannot know, we have bound him with chains of necessity. He is still hardly anything more than a physical being; let us continue to treat him as such."

With regard to the "natural arts" Rousseau says: "The first and most respectable of all the arts is agriculture. I should give blacksmithing the second place, carpentry the third, and so on." Nevertheless, since agriculture is incompatible with vagabond freedom, and blacksmithing untidy, he chooses carpentry for his pupil. "It is cleanly; it is useful; it may be carried on in the house; it calls upon the workman for dexterity and industry, and the usefulness of its products does not exclude elegance and taste." Rousseau deprecates all crafts that are unhealthy or effemi-

---

[1] Most children get over the Robinson Crusoe stage by the age of seven. Henry Thoreau was a notable exception. See his *Walden*, and cf. Tennyson's *Enoch Arden*.

nate, that deform the body, disgust the senses, or turn those who practise them into automata or machines. On the other hand, "if your pupil's genius should show a decided bent for the speculative sciences, then," he says, "I should not object to his being allowed to follow a craft conformable to his inclinations; to his learning, for example, to make mathematical instruments,[1] spectacles, telescopes, etc."

Rousseau, who may fairly claim the honor of being the father of manual training, would have every child learn a trade, and on this subject he makes some very pungent remarks. In reply to a fond mother who exclaims: "A handicraft for my son! My son an artisan! Do you think of such a thing, Sir?" he says, "Madam, I think better than you, who want to reduce him to a state in which he can never be anything but a lord, a marquis, a prince,[2] and perhaps some day less than nothing; while I want to confer on him a rank which he cannot lose, a rank which shall honor him at all times: I want to raise him to the dignity of a man, and, say what you will, he will have fewer equals in that rank than in those he may inherit from you." While admitting that the isolated man may do as he pleases, he insists that in society everybody must work. "Work is a duty indispen-

---

[1] Here he was evidently thinking of Spinoza.
[2] Cf. Burns' *A Man's a Man for a' That*: —

> "A king can mak a belted knicht,
> A marquis, duke, an' a' that;
> But an honest man's abune his micht;
> Guid faith! he mauna fa' that."

Burns derived not only the thought of this poem, but many other things, good and evil, from Rousseau.

L

sable for man in society. Rich or poor, strong or weak, the citizen who does not work is a scoundrel." And manual labor is to be preferred to every other, as affording the greatest freedom. "Of all occupations fitted to yield man a subsistence, that which comes nearest to the state of Nature is manual toil; of all conditions, the most independent of fortune and of men is that of the artisan. He depends only on his labor; he is as free as the ploughman is bound; for the latter is tied to his land, whose crop is at the mercy of others." . . . "By means of this land, he may be harassed in a thousand ways; whereas, if an attempt is made to harass an artisan, he can directly pull up his stakes, go off, and take his two arms with him."

In learning a trade, Émile can hardly fail to realize that coöperation in labor is valuable, and he may be allowed to make some reflections on this matter, and to think of men as united by industrial or material ties, whose meaning is within his reach; but no effort must be made to make him understand any other ties, since he has not the experience which would enable him to understand them. The force of this rule we shall see later.

In connection with the subject of industry, Rousseau takes occasion to air some of his economic and sociological doctrines; and, though the bearing of these upon his educational theories is but indirect, it is no less real and important on that account. We must, therefore, refer to them.

According to Rousseau, it is every man's first duty, *imposed by Nature*, to live. "Since, of all the aversions with which Nature inspires us, the strongest is the aversion to die, it follows that Nature allows a man to do anything that is absolutely necessary to preserve his life. The principles through which the virtuous man learns to despise his life, and sacrifice himself to his duty, are far removed from this primitive simplicity. Happy the peoples, among whom one can be good without effort, and just without virtue![1] If there is any wretched nation in the world in which it is not possible for every citizen to live without doing wrong, and where the citizens are rascals from necessity, it is not the wrong-doer that should be hanged, but he who forces him to become such." As if any one could be forced to do wrong against his will! This illogical and immoral doctrine has made dangerous fanatics without number, and encouraged criminals to hold society responsible for their crimes. It has, further, led to numerous attempts to moralize men by merely altering their surroundings, when the true method would have been to strengthen their wills through discipline, and to teach them that life without virtue is worthless.

Rousseau is opposed to inherited wealth. "The man or the citizen," he says, "whoever he be, has nothing to contribute to society but himself. All his other goods are in it in spite of him; and when a man is rich, he either does not enjoy his wealth, or the public enjoys it also. In the former case, he steals

[1] In other words, among whom goodness and justice are the result of blind instinct, and not of progressive moral effort or exertion of free choice. The whole of Rousseau's moral theory is here. Having himself no moral will, he tried to prove that men might be virtuous without such a thing.

from others what he deprives himself of; in the latter, he gives them nothing. Thus his social debt remains altogether undischarged, until he pays it with what is his own. 'But my father earned it, as an equivalent for services rendered to society' (you will say). Granted; he paid his debt, but not yours. You owe more to others than if you had been born penniless, because you were born favored. It is not just that what one man has done for society should relieve another from the debt which he owes it; for every one, owing his entire self to it, can pay only for himself, and no father can bequeath to his son the right to be useless to his fellows; and yet this is what, according to you, he does by bequeathing to him his wealth, which is the proof and price of his labor. He who eats in idleness what he has not himself earned, steals it; and a bondholder, whom the state pays for doing nothing, hardly differs, in my eyes, from a highway robber who lives at the expense of travellers." This specious nonsense, which contains the germs of the worst forms of socialism, derives its entire force from the fact that Rousseau, while granting a continuous personality to society, denies it to the family. But, surely, if society has a right to bequeath to future generations what it obtains through an exchange, the family, when it is the other party to the transaction, cannot be denied the same right. Such transmission does not remove wealth from society, and the mere possession of wealth, whether earned or inherited, has nothing whatever to do with a man's duty to serve society. The idler is a rotten and burdensome branch of the social tree, whether he be a penniless tramp or a landed millionaire! But socialism is hostile to the family.

Rousseau poured contempt upon the accumulated treasures of human experience, and upon all the means whereby they are made available to individual minds — books, study, schools, colleges, universities, social intercourse. Having himself very little knowledge and very little power of continuous thinking, he could not conceive that other men should desire to be unlike him. He despised "high thinking," and all attempts, through sustained inquiry and rigorous thought, to make the world rational, and to determine the place and destiny of man, as a rational being, in it. In the place of such thought, which is essentially universal and, therefore, social, he put vague sentiment and emotional intuition, which, like mystic experiences, depending upon temperament, are individual and unsocial. "Since our errors come from our judgments," he says, "it is clear that, if we never had to judge, we should never have to learn, and never be liable to deceive ourselves. We should be happier in our ignorance than we can be in our knowledge. Who denies that scholars know a thousand true things which the ignorant will never know? Are the scholars, therefore, nearer the truth? On the contrary, they get further from it as they go on, because, since the vanity of judging makes more progress than light does, every truth they learn is sure to come with a hundred false judgments. It is clear as daylight that the learned societies of Europe are merely public schools of lies; and it is very certain that there are more errors in the Academy of Sciences than among the whole Huron race.[1] Since the more men know, the more they deceive themselves, the only way to avoid error is ignorance. Do not judge, and you will never be duped. This is the lesson of Nature as well as of Reason. Apart from a very small number of very sensible relations between things and ourselves, we have naturally a profound indifference for all the rest. A savage would not turn his foot to see the working of the finest machine or all the prodigies of electricity. *What does it matter to me?* is the phrase most familiar to the ignorant, and most suitable to the wise." Though, in spite of this, Rousseau admits that men, when forced out of the savage state, must judge,[2] he, nevertheless, continually speaks of science, learning, and all that depends upon them, as degradations and necessary evils. In this way he favored obscurantism and superstition.

But alongside such evil teachings, Rousseau had others which were of a different nature. His attacks upon luxury, display, and the vain waste of wealth, and his eloquent praises of plain, simple, modest living, have laid humanity forever under deep obligations to him. Here the fervid, passion-tipped arrows of his rhetoric, which on other occasions turned men into anarchic fanatics, roused them from their dull, inertly blind lethargy, the inheritance from centuries of use and wont, and made millions of them, who had

[1] These judgments show what good reason Rousseau had to speak of the "vanity of judging," and to praise ignorance.

[2] It is needless to say that even the lowest savage, in so far as he is conscious, judges; for consciousness, which even the brutes possess, is nothing more or less than a complex of judgments. To be aware of a feeling is to make a judgment, or several.

been crouching before, and struggling after, wealth and conventional position, see that under their very hands and eyes were all the treasures of Nature, and the possibilities of a life which made these things seem contemptible. When, a century later, Emerson said, "Give me health and a day, and I will make the pomp of emperors ridiculous," he had been to school to Rousseau.[1]

According to Rousseau's plan, the three or four years of boyhood are to be passed in physical exercises, in learning a few necessary facts in regard to the physical world, and a few simple processes called the natural arts, and in drawing a few simple conclusions from such facts and processes. He says: "If I have made myself understood thus far, it will be readily imagined how, along with the habits of bodily exercise and manual training, I insensibly [2] impart to my pupil a taste for reflection and meditation, to counterbalance the sloth which would result from his indifference to men's judgments and from the calm of the passions. He must toil like a peasant and think like a philosopher, in order not to be as indolent as a savage. The great secret of education is to make bodily and mental exercises always serve as recreations from each other."

Looking back upon the progress made in this period, Rousseau says: "At first our pupil had only sensa-

[1] Indeed, as might easily be shown in detail, Emerson is, in the main, an American (moral) Rousseau, just as Wordsworth is an English one. "Good-bye, proud world, I'm going home," might have been written by Rousseau.

[2] So insensibly, indeed, that the reader fails to observe how, or that, it is done.

tions; now he has ideas.[1] At first he only felt; now he judges.[2] For from the comparison of several successive or simultaneous sensations, and from the judgment pronounced on them, arises a sort of mixed or complex sensation which I call idea."[3] "The manner of forming ideas," he continues, "is what imparts character to the human mind," and he gives a long list of mental characteristics arising from different ways of doing so. Then follows a passage so characteristic that it must be quoted. "Simple ideas are but compared sensations. *There are judgments in the simple sensations*, as well as in the complex sensations which I call ideas. In sensation the judgment is purely passive; it affirms[4] that what is felt is felt. In the perception, or idea, the judgment is active; it brings together, it compares, it determines[5] relations which the sense does not determine. This is all the difference; but it is great. Nature never deceives us; it is we[6] that deceive ourselves." It seems plain that, if the last statement is true, and self-deception is a vice, we are innately vicious.

But to return to Émile: he "has few acquirements in the way of knowledge; but those he has are truly his own: he knows nothing by halves. In the small number of things which he knows, and knows well,

---

[1] As if there were such things as simple sensations!

[2] As if he could feel without judging!

[3] Judgment, it seems, is a chemical action among sensations.

[4] Surely affirmation is an act, not a passion ($\pi\acute{a}\theta os$).

[5] By what means can it do this?

[6] If *we* are so completely opposed to Nature, what reason can there be for educating us according to Nature?

the most important is, that there are many which he does not know, but which he may know some time; many more which other men know, but which he will never know all his life, and an infinity of others which no man will ever know."[1] . . . "Émile has only natural and purely physical knowledge. He does not know even the name of history, or the meaning of metaphysics or morals. He knows the essential relations of men to things, but none of the moral relations of man to man. He knows little about how to generalize ideas, or to make abstractions.[2] He sees qualities common to certain bodies, without reasoning about these qualities themselves. He knows abstract extension by the help of geometrical figures, and abstract quantity by means of algebraic signs.[3] These figures and signs are the support of those abstractions upon which his senses rest. He does not try to know things through their nature, but only through the relations which interest him. He estimates what is foreign to him only by its relation to himself; but this estimation is accurate and certain. Fancy and convention play no part in it. He lays most stress upon what is most useful to him, and, never departing from this way of estimating, he sets no store by opinion. Émile is laborious, temperate, patient, firm, courageous.[4] His imagination, not having been

---

[1] That he, or anybody else, could arrive at such knowledge as this is a miracle surely.

[2] Rousseau does not see that every idea, whether simple or complex, involves both generalization and abstraction.

[3] It is certain that he would never know either by any such means.

[4] We find an exhibition of these virtues on p. 142.

fired in any way,[1] never magnifies dangers for him. He is sensible to few evils, and he can suffer with firmness,[2] because he has not learnt to wrangle with fate." . . . "In a word, Émile has all the virtues that relate to himself. In order to have also the social virtues, he merely requires to have the relations which call for them, and the light which his mind is now completely ready to receive. He thinks of himself without regard to others, and is content that others should not think of him. He asks nothing of anybody, and does not feel that he owes anything to anybody. He is also alone in human society, and relies only on himself.[3] As much as any one, he has a right to do this; for he is all that one can be at his age.[4] He has no errors, or only such as are inevitable. He has no vices, or only those against which no man is safe.[5] His body is healthy; his limbs agile; he is fair-minded and unprejudiced, heart-free and passionless. Self-love even, the first and most natural of all the passions, has hardly yet begun to stir. Without

---

[1] *Robinson Crusoe* seems to have proved somewhat firing. See p. 143.

[2] See above, p. 142.

[3] For what? we may ask. For his food and clothing? For the roof over his head? For self-guidance? If so, his tutor may vanish.

[4] This is certainly very wide of the truth.

[5] We have to take Rousseau's word for this. He has furnished us no proof for it. A boy of fifteen or sixteen, with no human relations but those of a puppet worked by the hidden wires of a magician tutor, cannot be said to have either virtues or vices. His will having never been called into exercise, he is altogether in a submoral condition, knowing neither good nor evil. At best, he is a well-trained animal.

disquieting any one, he has lived contented, happy, so far as Nature has allowed."[1]

Such is Émile, at the age of puberty, an altogether fantastic and impossible creature, a human automaton, neither man nor beast, utterly unloving and unlovable. Instead of being richly and plastically moulded by the manifold influences of society, he has been cast in a rigid, beggarly mould, by one man's cold caprice, calling itself natural necessity.

[1] No, as far as Rousseau's utterly false views of Nature have allowed. In fact, Émile has all the time been caged, watched, and trained in ignorance into complete artificiality.

CHAPTER VIII

ROUSSEAU'S EDUCATIONAL THEORIES

ADOLESCENCE

(*Émile*, Bk. IV.)

> A warmth within the breast would melt
> The freezing reason's colder part,
> And, like a man in wrath, the heart
> Stood up and answer'd, "I have felt."
> TENNYSON, *In Memoriam*, cxxiv.

In my dealing with my child, my Latin and Greek, my accomplishments, and my money stead me nothing; but as much soul as I have avails. If I am wilful, he sets his will against mine, one for one, and leaves me, if I please, the degradation of beating him by my superiority of strength.

EMERSON.

IT is the misfortune of all those people who despise or undervalue patient research, and careful reasoning from the same, that, when they undertake to write, they are forced to substitute for the true arrangements of science, specious schemes drawn from their own undisciplined imaginations. It was owing to such a misfortune that Rousseau was led to adopt the neat and pretty formula that, before the age of puberty the human being, having no sympathetic imagination, is guided entirely by selfish or egoistic instincts, and that only after that, and through the physical and emotional changes consequent upon it, he begins to manifest social instincts. These, he thinks, are awakened by the imagination, and the imagination, which enables us to go beyond ourselves and identify ourselves with others, springs up with the sexual instinct. That Rousseau should favor this view, is intelligible enough. So portentous and all-pervasive was the part played by the sexual passion in his own life, that it may fairly be said to have extended to every human relation which had any attraction for him. A relation without something of this meant nothing to him. This is the secret of his aversion to society, whose nobler relations have nothing to do with sexuality. And the theory itself is obtrusively untrue. Not only "is man by nature a political animal," but almost from the dawn of consciousness the child shows social sympathies, and gives evidence of lively imaginations. Very small children love their brothers, sisters, and playmates, and grieve when separated from them. Their attachment to their mothers and nurses is often deep and genuine.[1] Nor only so; but they learn quite early to understand social relations and to make moral distinctions. The latter may not always be correct; but that has nothing to do with the matter. Many children, at five or six, have very tender consciences, and are inconsolable when they think that they have done wrong, though they have no punishment to fear.[2]

[1] I knew a child of four who cried bitterly, because some one had said that his nurse, a very plain, almost grotesque, old woman, was not handsome.

[2] Rousseau, speaking of himself at the age of seven, says: "I had no idea of things, though *all the feelings* were already known

The chief aim of education during the period of adolescence is to "perfect reason by feeling."[1] When the sexual feelings have begun to stir, but, not having yet found, or concentrated themselves upon, their proper object, go out through imagination to all sentient beings indiscriminately, the time has come for the development and training of the social emotions,[2] — friendship, compassion, sympathy, etc. In the first place, every care is to be taken lest the sexual feelings should at once find their proper object, and, through imagination, concentrate themselves upon it, and Rousseau has some sensible remarks upon the way to prevent this. If they should at once find their object, the growing youth will, in all likelihood, become a selfish sensualist, cruel, thoughtless, and brutal, and never develop the social emotions at all.[3] If they do not, there will be an abundant overflow of warm friendliness. "A young man reared in simplicity is carried by the first movements of Nature

to me. I had conceived nothing; I had felt everything, and the *imaginary misfortunes* of my heroes drew from me a hundred times more tears in my childhood than even my own have ever made me shed." *Confessions*, Bk. I. Surely there is no lack of sympathy or imagination here!

[1] This completely inverts the order of fact. Feeling is primitive; reason merely makes distinctions in feeling. The world itself is only a complex of feelings distinguished and analyzed by reason, itself inherent in feeling.

[2] Emotion is that residue of primitive desiderant feeling (pleasure and pain) which has not been differentiated by perceptive or active organs, but which naturally connects itself with the feelings particularized by these, after they are formed.

[3] This was precisely Rousseau's own case. Here he could speak from bitter experience; and the sinner is by no means the worst preacher against sin.

toward tender and affectionate passions. His compassionate heart is moved by the sufferings of his kind; he starts with delight when his comrade comes back to him; his arms are able to find caressing embraces, his eyes to shed tears of tender emotion; he feels shame when he incurs displeasure, and regret when he causes offence. If the heat of his burning blood makes him quick, impatient, angry, the next moment all the goodness of his heart returns in the effusiveness of his repentance. He weeps, he sobs over the wound he has caused; with his own blood he would be glad to redeem that which he has shed; all his anger dies out; all his pride is humbled before the feeling of his fault. If he is offended himself, at the height of his fury, an excuse, a word, disarms him; he forgives the wrongs done him by others with the same good heart with which he repairs those he does to others." In an age when gush, embracing, weeping, and fainting were fashionable,[1] such a youth, no doubt, seemed in the highest degree admirable: he would hardly be the ideal of to-day among men of Germanic blood.

Rousseau sums up "the whole of human wisdom in the use of the passions" in two rules: (1) to feel the true relations of man, both in the species and in the individual; (2) to order all the affections of the soul in accordance with these relations. Only by follow-

---

[1] Hume, who had no superfluity of emotion, speaking of a scene with Rousseau, writes: "I assure you I kissed him and embraced him twenty times, with a plentiful effusion of tears. I think no scene of my life was ever more affecting." Burton, *Life of Hume*, II., 315.

ing these does man become moral. With a view to this Rousseau lays down three maxims, viz., —

(1) It is not in the power of the human heart to put itself in the place of those who are happier than we, but only of those who are more to be pitied.

(2) We pity in others only the sufferings from which we do not think ourselves safe.

(3) The pity which we feel for others' ills is not measured by the amount of those ills, but by what we suppose they suffer from them.

It might easily be shown that these maxims are untrue; but they are used by Rousseau to justify him in directing his pupil's newly awakened social sympathies to the sufferings, rather than to the joys, of humanity — to the poor and oppressed, rather than to the rich and overweening. And this furnishes him an opportunity, of which he makes masterly use, to compare the world of wealth and fashion with the world of poverty and simplicity — greatly to the advantage of the latter. He concludes that Émile must be removed from cities, where fashion, immodesty, and luxury contribute to sexual precocity and corruption, and taken to the country, to develop slowly in simplicity. Here he is still to be caged, guarded, and duped. If, in spite of all precautions, the passions prove incontrollable, he is to be taken to a hospital and shown the physical effects of unbridled lust in their worst form. At the same time every effort must be made to direct the young man's affections into broader and more peaceful channels. His tutor, hitherto so rigid, representing necessity, must now become his intimate friend, and strive to call out his affection for both himself and others. Under his guidance, Émile "must study society through men, and men through society," beginning with the study of the human heart. In this process, he will be able to distinguish between "the real and indestructible equality" due to Nature, and the chimerical and vain equality found in society, in which "the many are always sacrificed to the few, and public interests to private, and the specious names of justice and subordination always serve as instruments of violence and weapons of iniquity." But, in order that such study may not render him misanthropic and pessimistic, he must use other experiences besides his own, and be made acquainted with worthy people. His surroundings must be such that "he shall think well of those who live with him, and become so well acquainted with the world as to think everything that is done in it bad." "Let him know," says Rousseau, "that man is naturally good; let him feel it; let him judge his neighbor by himself; but let him see how society depraves and perverts men; let him find in their prejudices the source of all their vices; let him be brought to esteem each individual; but let him despise the multitude; let him see that all men wear pretty nearly the same mask; but let him also know that there are faces fairer than the masks that cover them." His personal experience may be widened and corrected by the study of history,[1] and especially of

[1] Much of what Rousseau says on the subject of history and the study of it is truly admirable, and deserves the most careful consideration on the part of educators. His estimate of Herodotus, Thucydides, Xenophon, Cæsar, Livy, Tacitus, etc., is entirely correct.

ancient history, which is simpler and truer than modern, as well as by the reading of well-written biographies, such as those of the inimitable Plutarch. But, after all, the best and most effective way of guiding the affections of a young man, and of making him acquainted with men, is to engage him in active benevolence. Kindly sentiments and noble words, which children learn at school, are impotent, compared with the experience that comes of kindly acts. "Direct your pupil," says Rousseau, "to all good actions that are possible for him; let the interest of the poor be always his interest; let him aid them, not only with his purse, but with his care; let him serve them, protect them, and devote his time to them; let him become their agent; he will never again, in all his life, fill so noble a place." Without troubling himself about the epithets which the public may apply to him, "he will do whatever he knows to be useful and good." . . . "He knows that his first duty is toward himself, that young people must be diffident, circumspect in their behavior, respectful to their elders, reticent and discreet in talking without occasion, modest in things indifferent, but bold in well-doing, and courageous in speaking the truth."[1] "To prevent pity from degenerating into weakness, it must be generalized and extended to the whole human race. Then we yield to it only in so far as it is in accord with justice, because, of all the virtues, justice is the one

[1] By what process the animal, self-centred Émile of sixteen becomes the bold philanthropist of eighteen, Rousseau says he is not bound to tell us, and we never find out; but the new Émile, if he could be made a reality, is certainly a most admirable creature, and deserves all the encomiums of his maker.

that contributes most to universal human well-being. Both from reason, and for our own sake, we must have pity on our race still more than on our neighbor; and it is a great cruelty toward men to have pity upon the wicked." In this way Émile acquires the two great virtues of humanity and justice.[1] Both are generalized pity.

Rousseau feels that his new ideal may seem impossible or fantastic to most people, who will say to him: "Nothing of what you suppose exists: young people are not made that way; they have such and such passions; they do this and that." To such he replies: "Just as if one were to deny that a pear-tree is ever a large tree, because we see only dwarfs in our gardens!"

There is still one more influence which may now be brought to bear, to calm the passions and give them beneficent direction, and that is Religion. Of this great subject no mention has thus far been made; it has played no part in Émile's early education. In recommending its introduction at the present stage, Rousseau gives his reasons for excluding it before. The most cogent of these is, that it could not with any effect have been introduced earlier, because the concepts with which it deals are unintelligible to the child. He blames Locke for maintaining that spirits should be studied before bodies, and declares that "this is the method of superstition," and "only serves

[1] Of course, this justice always remains an individual and subjective thing, a mere principle of knight-errantry, and cannot do otherwise, until it is embodied in a State capable of giving it universal effect. Plato showed this in his *Republic;* but Rousseau hated states.

to establish materialism," since, in trying to think spirits, children think only bodies, ghosts. "A spirit means but a body both to the common people and to children." ... "Every child who believes in God is, therefore, necessarily, an idolater, or, at least, an anthropomorphist; and, when once the imagination has seen God, the understanding rarely conceives him." And, even if we could impart to the child the notions current in philosophy, and could make him think a single substance, combining in itself the incompatible attributes of extension and thought,[1] we should not be much nearer the mark, or reach any comprehension of the theological "ideas of creation, annihilation, ubiquity, eternity, omnipotence, and those of the divine attributes." But not only are the conceptions of religion beyond the reach of a child; many of its teachings are apt to lead to the most fatal results. "*We must believe in God in order to be saved.* This dogma, wrongly understood, is the principle of bloody intolerance, and the cause of all those vain teachings which aim a mortal blow at human reason, by accustoming it to satisfy itself with words. To be sure, there is not a moment to be lost when eternal salvation is to be won; but, if it can be obtained by the mere repetition of certain words, I do not see what hinders us from peopling heaven with jackdaws and magpies, as well as with children." ... "What does the child, who professes the Christian religion,

---

[1] Here Rousseau shows some slight knowledge of the philosophies of Descartes and Spinoza, who held extension and thought to be incompatible. This is so far from being true that extension apart from thought is utterly inconceivable, as is also duration.

believe? What he conceives; and he conceives so little of what you say to him that, if you tell him the contrary, he will adopt it with equal readiness. The faith of children and many men is an affair of geography. Are they to be rewarded for being born in Rome, rather than in Mecca?" . . . "When a child says he believes in God, it is not in God that he believes. He believes Tom or Dick, who tells him that there is something which is called God." Since a child cannot believe in God, he cannot be punished for not doing so. "Reason tells us that a man is punishable only for the sins of his will, and that invincible ignorance can never be imputed to him as a crime." "Opinion triumphs in the matter of religion, more than in aught else. But, seeing that we set out to shake off its yoke in everything, and to allow no place for authority . . . in what religion shall we rear Émile? To what sect shall we assign the man of Nature. The answer, it seems to me, is very simple. We shall assign him to no sect; but we shall put him in a position to select that which the best use of his reason may lead him to."

Rousseau now undertakes to give an account of the religion of Nature or Reason; but, instead of this, really gives us his own beliefs, which sprang, not from Reason, but from tradition, sentiment, and desire. Moreover, instead of setting these forth in his own name, he puts them into the mouth of a humble and unfortunate Savoyard Vicar, whose traits are drawn from two men whom he had actually known.[1]

[1] See above, pp. 38, 40.

The Savoyard Vicar's *Confession of Faith*, though it would now be considered a very harmless production, made a great noise at the time of its appearance, and brought down upon Rousseau the odium and persecution of the whole religious world of France and Switzerland. It is nothing more or less than an attempt to prove what, some twenty years later, Kant, borrowing from Rousseau, called the three Postulates of the Pure Reason,— God, Freedom, and Immortality, — supposed to be the essentials of Natural Religion. Rousseau had been both a Catholic and a Protestant, had heard his father tell about his experiences with the Moslems in Constantinople, and had listened to the negative teachings of Voltaire and the Encyclopædists. The result was that, while sectarianism, with its exclusive dogmas, lost all meaning and authority for him, he still wished to retain what, listening to his heart, he was fain to consider the essentials of religion, and did his best to prove them true. His proofs, however, have no validity. In so far as they can be called proofs at all, they are mainly drawn from the writings of Dr. Samuel Clarke (died in 1729); but, in reality, they are mere feelings and desires translated into thoughts. The Vicar is made to say: "Impenetrable mysteries surround us on all sides;[1] they are above the sensible region; as a means of piercing them we think we have intelligence, and have only imagination. Through this imaginary world every one clears the path that seems good to him; no one can know whether his own leads to the goal. Nevertheless, we try to penetrate and to know everything.

[1] The greatest mystery of all is, how any one can know this.

The only thing we do not know how to do, is to be ignorant of what we cannot know."[1] . . . "The first result of these reflections was, that I learnt to limit my inquiries to what interested me immediately, to remain in profound ignorance of all the rest, and not even to take the trouble to doubt except about things which it was important for me to know"[2] . . . "Moreover, I realized that the philosophers, so far from delivering me from my useless doubts, would only multiply those that tormented me, without settling any of them. I, therefore, took another guide, and said: 'Let us consult the inner light;[3] it will not lead me so far astray as they do; or, at least, my error will be my own, and I shall be less depraved by following my own illusions than by trusting to their lies.'" . . . "Imagine all your philosophers, ancient and modern, having first exhausted their grotesque systems of force, chance, fatality, necessity, animated world, living matter, and materialism of every sort, and, after them, the illustrious Clarke, explaining the world, proclaiming, at last, the Being of beings and the dispenser of things; with what universal admiration, with what unanimous applause would this system have been received — a system so grand, so consoling, so sublime, so calculated to uplift

---

[1] In these sentences we have the germs both of **Kantian Criticism** and of **Huxleyan Agnosticism**.

[2] Good; but what *is* important for us to know?

[3] "They tell us," he says elsewhere, "that conscience is the result of prejudice; yet I know, *from my experience*, that it insists upon following the order of Nature, in opposition to all the laws of men." Here we have complete **subjectivism, individualism, and anarchism.**

the soul, to furnish a foundation for virtue, and, at the same time, so luminous, so simple, and, it seems to me, offering fewer things incomprehensible to the human mind than there are absurdities in any other system!" . . . "Having thus, within myself, the love of truth as my only philosophy, and, as my only method, an easy and simple rule, which relieves me from the vain subtlety of arguments, I resumed, in accordance with this rule, the examination of those parts of knowledge which interested me, being determined to accept, as evident, all those to which, *in the sincerity of my heart*, I could not refuse my assent; as true all those that might seem to me to have a necessary connection[1] with the former, and to leave all the rest uncertain, without either rejecting or accepting them, and without bothering myself to explain them, seeing that they lead to nothing useful in practice." Proceeding on the lines of Descartes, Rousseau comes to this: "I exist, and I have senses, through which I am affected.[2] This is the first truth that strikes me, and to which I am forced to assent."

It would be vain to waste time on these crudities. They are not due to any accurate thinking, or to any real, enlightened desire for the truth, but to an effort to justify a lazy, intellectual habit, in behalf of a foregone scheme of sensuous, unsocial life. If sectarian beliefs are a matter of geography, these emotional prejudices are matters of both geography and individual

---

[1] It requires considerable philosophy to find out what is a necessary connection, and what "necessary" means.

[2] Yes; but what is the meaning of 'I,' 'exist,' 'senses,' 'affected'? To tell that requires a subtle philosophy.

temperament. Neither Rousseau's acquaintance, Helvétius, nor any Singhalese Buddhist would have found any difficulty in refusing assent to Rousseau's self-evident truths. He may well be spoken of as a mystic voluptuary,—

> "Quenching all wonder with omnipotence,
> Praising a name with indolent piety."[1]

We are interested in his scheme only because it furnishes the method by which Émile is to be led to religion, to that view of higher things supposed to be necessary for the direction of his passions and imagination. "By developing the natural," says Rousseau, "we have been able to control his nascent sensibility; by cultivating the reason, we have regulated it. Intellectual objects moderated the expression of sensible objects. By rising to the principle of things, we have withdrawn him from the dominion of the senses. It was a simple matter to rise from the study of Nature to the search for its author."

The recently unimaginative, unreflective Émile, being thus daily sentimentalized, will be very unlike other youths. "You always imagine him," says Rousseau, "like your young men, always heedless, always petulant, flighty, wandering from fête to fête, from amusement to amusement, without being able to adhere to anything. You will laugh to see me make a contemplative being, a philosopher,[2] a true theologian, out of an ardent, quick, high-tempered, high-spirited young man, at the most ebullient time of his

[1] George Eliot, *Spanish Gypsy*, Bk. I.
[2] If he had submitted to this indignity, Rousseau would have disowned him.

life.". . . "I, comparing my pupil with yours, find that they can hardly have anything in common." . . . "Yours think they escape from childhood only by shaking off all sort of yoke; they then make up for the long constraint to which they have been subjected, as a prisoner does, who, when delivered from his fetters, puts forth, shakes, and bends his limbs. Émile, on the contrary, is proud to become a man, and to submit to the yoke of nascent reason. His body, already formed, has no need of the old movements, and begins to stop of itself, whilst his mind, half-developed, now, in turn, seeks to soar. Thus, while the age of reason is, for the former, the age of license, it becomes for the latter the age of reasoning."

But, in spite of all efforts to drain off into side channels the rising tide of sexual instinct, the time at last comes when this can no longer be done. "From this moment," says Rousseau, your ward, "though still your disciple, is no longer your pupil. He is your friend; he is a man. Treat him henceforth as such." . . . "Hitherto you have got nothing from him except by force or wiles: authority and the law of duty were unknown to him; he had to be forced or duped, before he would obey you." . . . "In order to guide an adult, you must do the very opposite of all that you have done in order to guide a child." In accordance with this, Émile is now to be informed of all that has been hitherto concealed from him — the purpose and method of his past education, the dupery that has been practised on him, the course he has to pursue in the future, and the perils that await him, especially those arising from his own passions. In regard to these he is now to receive clear and earnest instruction. To protect him from passion-suggested imaginings, he is to be withdrawn from all lonely, sedentary, lazy occupations, as well as from the society of women and young men, and made to engage in vigorous pursuits, such as hunting, which will not only occupy his mind, but tire out his body. At the same time the sexual relation is, in various ways, to be surrounded with a halo of sacramental awe, as the portal to supreme bliss. "Thereupon," says Rousseau, "I will call the Eternal Being, whose work he is, to attest the truth of my words; I will make him judge between Émile and me; I will mark the place where we are, the rocks, the woods, the mountains that surround us, as monuments of his pledges and mine. I will throw into my eyes, my voice, my gestures, the enthusiasm and the ardor with which I wish to inspire him. Then I shall speak, and he will listen to me. I shall melt, and he will be moved. By thus suffusing myself with the sanctity of my duties, I shall render his more worthy of respect; I shall strengthen and animate my reasoning with images and figures; I shall not be prolix and diffuse in cold maxims, but abounding in overflowing feelings; my reason will be grave and sententious; but my heart will never have said enough. Then, in showing him all that I have done for him,[1] I shall show him that I have done it for myself: he will see in my tender affection the reason of all my care. What surprise, what agitation I shall cause him, by

[1] The tutor, it must be remembered, gives his services gratuitously.

this sudden change of language! Instead of belittling his soul by continually talking to him about his own interests, I shall henceforth talk to him of mine, and I shall touch him more deeply. I shall inflame his young heart with all the feelings of friendship, generosity, and gratitude which I have already called forth, and which are so sweet to nourish. I shall press him to my bosom, shedding over him tears of tenderness: I shall say to him: 'You are my property, my child, my work; from your happiness I expect mine: if you frustrate my hopes, you steal twenty years of my life, and you cause the unhappiness of my declining years.' It is in this way that one can make a young man listen to him, and engrave on the bottom of his heart the remembrance of what one says to him."

Alas for Émile, if he can be caught by any such lachrymose discharge as this! It is needless to say that it is at once ungenerous and immoral, as all attempt to guide a human being by any other motive than moral insight always is. If Émile were properly educated, he would repel all such suggestions with scornful indignation, or, if he had any sense of humor, with pitying laughter. Instead of this, he is made to reply: "O my friend, my protector, my master! resume the authority which you proposed to lay down at the moment when it was most necessary that you should retain it. Thus far you have possessed it only through my weakness; now you shall possess it through my will; and it will be all the more sacred to me for that reason. Defend me from all the enemies that assail me, and especially from those that I carry within myself, and that betray me. Watch over your work, that it may remain worthy of you. I wish to obey your laws; I wish it always: it is my constant will. If ever I disobey you, it will be in spite of myself. Make me free, by protecting me against my passions, which do me violence; save me from being their slave, and compel me to be my own master, by obeying, not my senses, but my reason."

Émile, having thus, like a coward, voluntarily renounced his moral autonomy, for the sake of being protected from himself, reverts once more to automatism. "To be sure," says Rousseau, "I leave him the semblance of independence; but his subjection to me is more complete than ever, because he wishes it to be so. So long as I could not make myself master of his will, I remained master of his body. Now I sometimes leave him to himself, because I always govern him. When I leave him, I embrace him, and say in a confident tone: 'Émile, I entrust you to my friend; I commit you to his upright heart: he will be responsible to me for you.'" On the very next page, however, he says: "Do not leave him alone day or night; sleep, at the very least, in his room. See that he does not go to bed until he is overcome with sleep, and that he gets up as soon as he awakes." In this state of complete tutelage, his imagination is to be filled with fairy-tales of his future spouse, and glowing descriptions of the idyllic life of love[1] that

---

[1] Here is Rousseau's notion of love: "What is true love itself but chimera, lie, illusion? We love far more the image which we form than the object to which we apply it. If we saw the object of our love exactly as it is, there would be no more love in the world."

is in store for him and her. Such fanciful pictures will destroy in him all taste for real women, until he can be induced to believe that he has met one corresponding to his chimera. In order that he may do this, he is now, for the first time, to be introduced into society; and Rousseau draws a vivid contrast between him, in his noble, savage simplicity and absence of self-consciousness, and the ordinary youth of his time, with his vanity and veneer of politeness. In this connection he quotes, from his friend Duclos, a few sentences which may here be transcribed: —

"The most unfortunate effect of ordinary politeness is, that it teaches the art of dispensing with the virtues which it imitates. Let education inspire us with humanity and kindliness, and we shall either have politeness, or else no need for it.

"If we have not that politeness which is marked by the graces, we shall have that which marks the upright man and the citizen; we shall not need to have recourse to falseness.

"Instead of being artificial in order to please, it will be enough to be kind: instead of being false, in order to flatter others, it will be enough to be indulgent.

"Those with whom we stand in such relations will be neither puffed up with pride nor corrupted. They will only be grateful and become better."

Émile, thrown into society, will — one does not see how — find himself completely at home in it, and will at once earn respect and confidence, although he have no brilliant qualities. In studying men, "he will often have occasion to reflect on what flatters or shocks the human heart, and so he will find himself philosophizing on the principles of taste — a study suitable for this stage in his career." Rousseau's æsthetic theory is delightfully simple: "The further we go in search of definitions of taste," he says, "the further we go astray. Taste is simply the faculty of judging what pleases or displeases the greater number." Taste depends, at bottom, on innate sensibility; but three conditions are necessary for its cultivation. "*First*, one must live in numerous societies in order to make many comparisons. *Second*, there must be societies devoted to amusement and indolence; for in societies devoted to business the rule is not pleasure, but interest. *Third*, there must be societies in which the inequality of conditions is not too great, and in which pleasure, rather than vanity, prevails. Where this is not the case, fashion stifles taste, and people seek no longer what pleases, but what distinguishes." In seeking to cultivate his taste, that is, the art of pleasing, Émile will look to Nature, rather than to Culture. "There is at present no civilized place in the world where the general taste is worse than in Paris." . . . "Those who guide us are the artists, the great, the rich; and what guides them is their interest or their vanity. The rich, in order to display their riches, and the others, in order to profit thereby, vie with one another in seeking out new means of expense. In this way excessive luxury establishes its empire, and makes people love what is difficult and costly. Then the pretended beautiful, far from imitating Nature, is beautiful only because it thwarts Nature. This is why luxury and bad taste are inseparable. Wherever taste is expensive, it is false."

But "it is chiefly in the intercourse between the two sexes that taste, good or bad, is formed." . . . "Consult woman's taste in physical things, things dependent on the judgment of the senses, men's in things moral, dependent on the judgment of the understanding." . . . "Inasmuch as it is necessary to please men, in order to serve them; and the art of writing is anything but a useless study, when it is employed to make them listen to the truth," Émile will now study the best literary models, and especially the works of the ancients. "In eloquence, in poetry, and in every species of literature, as well as in history, he will find them abounding in things, and sober in judgment, whereas our authors speak much and say little." In view of this, he will now learn Latin, Greek, and Italian. "Latin he must learn in order to know French well." . . . "These studies will now be amusements for him, and he will profit by them all the more that he is not forced to them." He will thus "go back to the sources of pure literature," and learn to despise "the sewerage in the reservoirs of modern compilers, journals, translations, dictionaries; he will cast a glance at all that, and bid it good-bye forever." As to the babblings of academies, they will merely be fun to him. "My principal object," says Rousseau, in conclusion, "in teaching him to feel and love the beautiful in all its forms, is to fix his affections and his tastes, to prevent his natural appetites from degenerating, and himself from one day seeking in his riches the means of happiness which he ought to find nearer home."

Having thus become acquainted with society, and

learnt the art of pleasing, Émile is now, at last, in a position to look out for a wife in good earnest. "Therefore, good-bye, Paris, famous city, city of noise, smoke, and mud, where the women no longer believe in honor, nor the men in virtue! Good-bye, Paris! We are in quest of love, happiness, innocence. We shall never be far enough from you."

Lest we should misunderstand the meaning of these last words, Rousseau has taken care, in the closing pages of this book, to give us his own ideal of life. It is simply that of an accomplished voluptuary, whose aim is to get as much real pleasure (*volupté réelle*) as possible out of life, and who, therefore, avoids everything that would entail envy, strife, and unpleasantness, all formalities that would cause tedium, and all excesses that would diminish the power of sensual enjoyment. He tells us, indeed, that he is here speaking "not of moral possessions, which relate to the dispositions of the soul, but to those of sensuality and real pleasure, in which prejudice and opinion have no part." We know, however, through his *Confessions* and otherwise, that morality meant nothing to him but a careful calculation of the possibilities of undisturbed sensual enjoyment. We may fairly conclude, therefore, that the aim of Émile's education, thus far, has been to prepare him, not for a life of earnest, determined moral struggle and self-sacrifice, but for a life of quiet, cleanly, assured sensuous delight; not for a life of active enterprise, but for a life of passive dalliance.

CHAPTER IX

ROUSSEAU'S EDUCATIONAL THEORIES

YOUTH

(*Émile*, Bk. V.)

Willst du genau erfahren was sich ziemt,
So frage nur bei edeln Frauen an.
GŒTHE.

And manhood fused with female grace,
  In such a sort, the child would twine
  A trustful hand, unask'd, in thine,
And find his comfort in thy face.
TENNYSON, *In Memoriam*, CIX.

Love seeketh not its own.
PAUL.

ROUSSEAU's Émile is now a young man, whose chief purpose is to find a suitable wife, to complete his sensuous happiness. Rousseau, like all sensualists, has a low opinion of women. They live in their senses, and not in their understanding. While man must be active and strong, woman must be passive and weak. "The one must necessarily have will and power; it is enough if the other offer but little resistance." . . . "It follows that woman is made to please man." . . . "If woman is made to please man and to be subjugated, she must make herself agreeable to him, instead of provoking him: her violence lies in her charms." . . . "The minds of women correspond exactly to their constitution. Far from being ashamed of their weakness, they glory in it. Their tender muscles are without resistance, they pretend not to be able to lift the lightest burdens; they would be ashamed to be strong. Why? It is certainly not for the sake of seeming delicate; it is from a far shrewder precaution: they are preparing, a long way beforehand, excuses for being weak, and the right to be so on occasions." . . . "Thus all the education of women must have relation to men. To please them, to be useful to them, to rear them when they are young, to tend them when they are grown, counsel and console them, to make their lives pleasant and sweet, — these are the duties of women in all times, and what they ought to learn from earliest childhood." . . . "Woman is a coquette by profession; but her coquetry changes form and object according to her views. Let us regulate these views by those of nature, and woman will have the education that befits her." She is different from man and has different functions; she must, therefore, receive a different education. Rousseau has much to say about these differences. They rest largely on the notion that command and independence belong to man; obedience and dependence upon woman. While he is to be taught to be strong, and defiant of public opinion, she must learn to be agreeable, and sensitive to such opinion. "Opinion is virtue's tomb among men, and its throne among women." At the same time, a girl's education must, in many respects, resemble that of a boy. She must at first have plenty of exercise and frolic. "All that confines and constrains Nature is in bad taste; this is as true of the decorations of the body as of those of the mind. Life, health, reason, well-being, must take precedence of everything. There is no grace without ease; delicacy is not languor; one need not be unhealthy in order to please." The amusements of a girl will be gentler than those of a boy, aiming at refinement rather than strength. Instead of learning to read and write, as girls usually do, she will play with dolls, sew, embroider, make lace, and paint flowers, fruit, and such things, carefully avoiding figures and landscapes. A little arithmetic will not be out of place. "Girls must be wide-awake and laborious; more than that, they must be early subjected to repression (*gêne*). This misfortune, if it is one for them, is inseparable from their sex; and they can free themselves from it only by exposing themselves to suffer others more cruel. All their lives they will be subjected to the most continuous and severe repression, that of propriety. From the first they must be exercised in constraint, so that it may never cost them anything; and taught to overcome all their fancies, in order to subject them to the will of others." They must be educated at home, under the eyes of their parents, and "never for one instant in their lives be allowed not to feel the bridle." "Accustom them to be interrupted in the midst of their games, and to be carried off to other occupations without a murmur." . . . "From this habitual constraint there results a docility, which women have need of all their lives, since they never cease to be subjected either to a man or to the judgments of men, without their ever being allowed to set themselves above these judgments. The first and most important attribute of a woman is sweetness. Being made to obey an imperfect being like man, often so full of vices, and always so full of faults, she must early learn to submit even to injustice, and to bear the misdeeds of a husband without complaining." . . . "She must never scold." Her weapon of defence is cleverness or address. If she were not artful, she would be man's slave. She must, therefore, cultivate artfulness. "Let us not destroy the instruments of happiness, because the wicked use them for mischief." A girl is to cultivate taste, but to be simple in her adornments. Setting fashion at defiance, she will consider only what is becoming to her, what makes her pleasing. She must not try to be a mediæval saint, knowing only the command *Ora et labora*, nor "live like a grandmother. She must be lively, hearty, merry; she must sing and dance to her heart's content, and enjoy all the innocent pleasures of her years." Her singing must not be of the professional sort, but simple and natural; and she may learn to play her own accompaniments "without being able to read a single note." Since "the talent for conversation takes the first place in the art of pleasing," she must early acquire it. "While a man speaks what he knows, a woman speaks what pleases. In order to talk, the one requires knowledge, the other taste; the object of the one should be useful things, that of the other, agreeable things." . . . "We ought not, therefore, to stop the chatter of girls, as we would do that of boys, by the question: What is the use of that? but with this one, which is not more easy to answer: What effect will that produce?" . . . "They must make it a rule never to say anything but what is agreeable to those with whom they talk." At the same time, they must never lie.

Religion ought to be taught earlier to girls than to boys, — the religion of their parents. "Since the conduct of woman is enslaved to public opinion, her belief is enslaved to authority. Every girl ought to follow the religion of her mother, and every wife that of her husband. If this religion be false, the docility which makes the mother and the daughter submit to the order of Nature wipes out, in God's sight, the sin of error. Being incapable of judging for themselves, they ought to accept the decision of their fathers and husbands, as that of the Church." . . . "Since authority must regulate the religion of women, it is of less importance to explain to them the grounds you have for believing than to set clearly before them what you do believe." . . . "When you explain articles of faith to them, let it be done in the form of direct instruction. In replying, they must say only what they think, not what has been dictated to them. All the answers in the catechism are preposterous: it is the scholar instructing the teacher. They are even lies in the mouths of children." In religious instruction no notice should be taken of those dogmas which have no direct bearing on practice. "That a virgin is the mother of her Creator; that she gave birth to God, or merely to a man with whom God united himself; that the Father and the Son have the same substance, or only a similar one; that the Holy Spirit proceeds from one of the two who are the same, or from the two conjointly — I do not see that the decision of these questions, in appearance essential, is of any more importance to the human race than to know on what day of the moon Easter ought to be celebrated, whether we ought to say the rosary, fast, eat fish and eggs, speak Latin or French in church, adorn the walls with images, say or listen to mass; and have no wife of one's own. Let everybody think about these things as he pleases. I do not know how far they may interest other people; they do not interest me at all. But what interests me, and others like me, is, that every one should know that there exists an arbiter of the lot of men, whose children we all are, who orders us all to be just, to love one another, to be kindly and merciful, to keep our agreements with everybody, even with our enemies and his; that the apparent happiness of this life is nothing; that after it there comes another, in which this Supreme Being will be the rewarder of the good and the judge of the wicked. These are the dogmas which it is important to teach young people, and to impress upon all citizens. Any one who contests them certainly deserves punishment; he is the disturber of order, and the enemy of society. Whoever goes beyond them, and seeks to subject us to his private opinions, comes to the same point by an opposite path: to establish order after his fashion, he disturbs the peace; in his forward pride he makes himself the interpreter of the Divinity; he demands, in his name, the homage and respect of men, and puts himself, as far as he can, in the place of God. He ought to be punished for sacrilege, if not for intolerance."[1] "Ignore, therefore," he continues, "all those mysterious dogmas which are for us words without ideas." . . . "Keep your children always within the narrow circle of those dogmas which relate to morality. Persuade them that there is nothing useful for us to know but what teaches us to do good. Do not make your daughters theologians or reasoners; . . . accustom them to feel themselves under the eyes of God, to take him as witness of all their actions and thoughts, of their virtue and pleasures; to do good without ostentation, because he loves it; to suffer evil without a murmur, because he will one day make it up to them;[2] finally, to be, during all the days of their life, what they would wish to have been, when they shall appear before him. This is the true religion; this is the only one that is liable to neither abuse, impiety, nor fanaticism. Let others preach sublimer ones as much as they please; I know of none but this."

But though, according to Rousseau, women are destitute of reason, such as would enable them to discuss questions of theology and ethics, yet they have something which takes its place. "There exists, for the whole human race, a rule anterior to opinion." . . . "It judges prejudice even; and it is only in so far as the judgment of men agrees with it, that this judg-

---

[1] This somewhat lengthy quotation has been made with the view of bringing out three things: (1) Rousseau's religious views; (2) his ethical sanctions, which are of a supernatural sort; (3) his religious intolerance, which matches even that of Calvin, and reveals the unphilosophical fanatic. Cf. p. 215.

[2] In ethics Rousseau never rises above this other-worldly self-interest. Of nobility, as an end, he has no notion.

ment can be authoritative for us. This rule is the inner sentiment." It follows from this, that the moral guide of women is, after all, a subjective feeling. How treacherous this may be, when separated from reason, hardly needs to be remarked. It must be admitted, however, that Rousseau rarely appeals to it. Religion and ethics are with him mostly matters of rhetoric; his real sanctions are always happiness and self-interest. He is a hedonist of the first rank. "The consideration of duty," he says, "has force only in so far as it is supported by motives that prompt us to fulfil it."

We are now introduced to Sophie, the young woman who, for a long time, has been in process of education on these principles, with a view to union with Émile. She is, for a woman, what Émile is, for a man. She has had the education of Nature. Her parents, people of good family, and once rich, having lost the bulk of their property, have retired to a charming situation in the country, where they have led a simple and retired life, and reared their only daughter. This daughter is described to us at great length. She is good-natured, sensitive, imaginative, attractive but not pretty; she has a sweet expression, a fine complexion, a white hand, a tiny foot, and a touching physiognomy. She is fond of adornment, and dresses well. "Her attire is very modest in appearance, and very coquettish in fact." She has natural talents. She sings sweetly and tastefully; she walks lightly and gracefully; she makes pretty curtsies. She is well versed in all feminine occupations; she cuts and makes her own clothes, and manufactures lace—

"because there is no other occupation that imparts a more agreeable attitude, or in which the fingers are plied with more grace and lightness"! She can keep house; but, though she is fond of good things to eat, she does not like cooking, because it is not altogether cleanly. In this matter she is extremely fastidious. "She would rather let a whole dinner burn up than have a spot on her cuff." She likes pastry and sweets, but cares little for meat. She is agreeable, without being brilliant, gay without being boisterous, sensitive, but easily pacified and forgiving. She has a simple, rational religion, with few dogmas, and yet fewer devotional exercises. She devotes her life to serving God by doing good; she loves virtue with devouring passion — because there is nothing so beautiful as virtue. She knows all the duties of both sexes, and longs to make one upright man happy. She never speaks ill of any one, and never uses vain forms of politeness. She hates officious gallantry, and, though rather short, does not wear high heels. She receives the flirtatious compliments of young men "with an ironical applause which disconcerts." When she reaches marriageable age, she receives an instructive lecture from her father, and makes a confidante of her mother. She reads by chance Fénelon's *Télémaque* and falls in love with the hero, whose image makes all the young men she knows distasteful to her. In this situation she exclaims: "Let us not think that a lovable and virtuous man is only a chimera. He exists, he lives; he is perhaps looking for me — looking for a soul that can love him. But what is he? Where is he? I do not know; he is not among those whom I have seen, and surely will not be among those whom I shall see. O mother! why have you made virtue too dear to me? If I can love but it, the fault is yours rather than mine!"

She is now ready for Émile, and Émile is ready for her. They must, therefore, be brought together, but without their knowing that this is done intentionally. Everything is arranged behind their backs, and they, with all their supposed penetration, — now heightened by budding passion, — are mere innocent dupes. Émile's tutor, as the representative of Nature, claims the sole right of arranging for his marriage. "It is not I," he says, "who destine them for each other; it is Nature; my business is to discover her choice. I say 'my business,' and not his father's. In entrusting his son to me, he yields me his place, puts my right in place of his own: it is I who am Émile's real father; it is I who have made him a man. I should have refused to bring him up, had I not been permitted to marry him according to his own, that is, to my, choice."

Before bringing the future lovers together, Rousseau enters, at some length, into the conditions of a happy marriage, the semi-sensuous, dalliant delights of which are to him the all-in-all of life.[1] The details of these do not concern us here; but three points may be noted. He holds (1) that, while natural love should be the

[1] It is impossible not to feel, in all Rousseau's descriptions of wedded bliss, that he has before his mind his own life with Madame de Warens at Les Charmettes. He seems to be continually comparing that with his life with Thérèse, and asking by what means the former could be rendered permanent. The abode of Sophie's parents is just Les Charmettes. See p. 45.

determining motive of marriage, similarity of tastes and culture should not be disregarded; (2) that great beauty should be avoided, rather than sought, by a man in wooing; (3) that a woman with anything like a literary or scientific education is to be avoided like a pestilence. "A woman of culture" (*bel esprit*), he says, "is the plague of her husband, her children, her friends, her servants, everybody."

At the proper moment, Émile and his tutor joyously shake the dust of corrupt and corrupting Paris from their feet, and start on a foot-tour, without any fixed destination. Rousseau's description of this tour, and its manifold fresh, simple delights, is masterly. Perhaps no man that ever lived knew the sensuous charms of free Nature, and of vagabond freedom, so well as he, and no one ever described them in such glowing terms. After a few days, the wanderers lose their way (they are always conveniently doing that!) and have to appeal to a kindly peasant for food. When they part with him, he says: "If God had graciously guided you to the other side of the hill, you would have had a better reception; you would have found a house of peace — such charitable, such good people! They have no better heart than mine; but they are better off, although I am told they were much more so formerly. . . . They don't suffer, thank God, and all the country round is better for what is left." Émile, of course, comes up to the occasion, being a

---

[1] It is needless to say that this speech has been prearranged with a view to producing upon Émile a favorable impression of these people. It implies in Rousseau a correct knowledge of suggestive psychology.

most satisfactory puppet. "At these words about good people, Émile's kind heart expands. 'Master,' he says, looking at me, 'let us go to this house whose owners are blessed in the neighborhood. I should be glad to see them; perhaps they would be glad to see us too. I am sure they will receive us well. If they are ours, we shall be theirs.'" They, accordingly, repair to the house, and are most graciously received, so graciously, indeed, that Émile, so often duped for his benefit, exclaims, in the simplicity of his heart: "Why, one would think we had been expected! How right the peasant was! What attention! What kindness! What foresight! And for strangers! I could imagine myself in the time of Homer." It is needless to say that we are in the home of Sophie, for whom Émile's imagination has so long been prepared.

Sophie duly appears, behaves properly and sweetly, and the two fall in love with each other almost at first sight. The details of their courtship do not belong here. They form a charming idyl, one of the most charming ever written, which has only one drawback: the characters are all puppets, whose wires are in the hands of the all-knowing, all-designing tutor. Émile and this tutor establish themselves in a town some two leagues distant from Sophie's home, and she, with the consent of her parents, allows them to visit her about twice a week. The tutor takes care that things shall not proceed very rapidly; indeed, he prolongs the season of wooing as much as he can, on the ground that love's "supreme bliss is a hundred times sweeter to look forward to than to enjoy." Meanwhile, Émile is spending his time in examining the surrounding country, in entering into relations with peasants, learning their needs, giving them aid and instruction, showing his ability in ploughing and in the arts of agriculture, earning his daily bread by working as a carpenter, and in playing Lord Bountiful generally. At the end of two months, an engagement takes place, and Émile is in the seventh heaven. He still remains in Sophie's neighborhood, and is now allowed to visit her more frequently. He sings, plays, races, and dances with her, mends her piano, teaches her philosophy,[1] physics, mathematics, history; indeed, everything he knows. They draw and paint together, and decorate Sophie's home with the results. At the end of three months, Émile fondly thinks that the consummation of all his hopes is near. But alas! his tutor, whom he has undertaken to obey, has a bitter disappointment in store for him. He must postpone the realization of his dearest wishes, control his passion, and leave Sophie for two years. He is not ready to marry. He does not know either himself or Sophie sufficiently; he has not sufficiently realized the duties of husband and father; he has almost no acquaintance with social and political relations. The tutor, who has hitherto spoken and acted like an optimistic Epicurean, declaring that his sole desire was to secure the happiness of his pupil,[2] now suddenly changes his tone and adopts that of a severe, pessimistic Stoic.

[1] Here Rousseau is careful to tell us that "the art of thinking is not foreign to women; but they must do no more than graze the sciences of reasoning."

[2] He says, in so many words: "I have not educated my Émile to desire or to wait, but to enjoy."

Man must rise above his natural desires and passions, and take Reason for his guide. He must detach himself from all dependence upon transient and earthly things, and be prepared for every change of fortune. The man "who has no laws but the wishes of his heart, and can resist no desire," is guilty of a crime. "Who, then, is the virtuous man? He who can govern his affections; for then he follows reason and conscience. He does his duty, and nothing can make him swerve from it." . . . "All the passions are good, so long as we are masters of them; all are bad, as soon as we become enslaved to them." . . . "All the feelings which we master are legitimate; all those which master us are criminal. A man is not to blame for loving his neighbor's wife, so long as he keeps his unfortunate passion in subjection to the law of duty; he is to blame for loving his own wife, when he goes so far as to sacrifice everything to this love." . . . "If you wish to live virtuous and wise, let your heart cleave only to the beauty that perishes not, . . . extend the law of necessity to things moral; learn to lose what may be taken away; to give up all at the command of virtue, and to place yourself beyond the reach of events." . . . "Then you will be happy in spite of fortune, and self-controlled in spite of passion. Then you will find in the possession of transient things a delight which nothing can disturb. You will possess them, without their possessing you, and you will come to feel that man, from whom everything drops away, enjoys only that which he knows how to lose." Émile is, of course, outraged, at such unwonted talk, and declares that he cannot leave

Sophie without being "a traitor, a scoundrel, and a perjurer." The tutor lets him vent his first indignation, and then continues, saying, among other things: "Sensual happiness is transient." . . . "The imagination, which tricks out the objects of desire, leaves them bare, when they become objects of possession. Except the one self-existent Being, there is nothing beautiful but what is not. If your present condition could have lasted always, you would have found the supreme good. But all that relates to man withers as he does; all is finite, all is transient in human life." . . . "Not yet trained to battle with himself, not yet accustomed to desire one thing and will another, the young man refuses to yield; he resists and disputes." He does not see why he must go away; or, if he must go, why he cannot make sure of Sophie, by marrying her first. The tutor points out to him the impropriety of leaving a wife, and, when Émile still recalcitrates, puts an end to further dispute by a fiat of authority. "Since you will not obey reason," he says, "then recognize another master. You have not forgotten the compact which you entered into with me. Émile, you must leave Sophie: I desire it." At this the young man yields, and their departure is fixed for a week later.

Sophie and her parents have to be won over to the new scheme, and this is a matter of no small difficulty. Sophie tries to bear up under her sad trial, but in secret weeps and wails in spite of herself. The tutor comforts and reassures her; and one day says to her: "Sophie, exchange books with Émile. Give him your *Télémaque*, in order that he may learn to be like him; and let him give you the *Spectator*, which you are so fond of reading. Study in it the duties of virtuous women, and think that in two years these duties will be yours." The lovers at last part in this fashion: "Émile, impatient, ardent, agitated, beside himself, shrieks, sheds torrents of tears on the hands of father, mother, and daughter, embraces with sobs all the people in the house, and repeats the same things over and over again a thousand times, with a disorder that would excite laughter on any other occasion.[1] Sophie, sad, pale, with lustreless eye and mournful look, remains quiet, utters not a word, weeps not, sees no one, not even Émile. In vain he takes her hands, and clasps her in his arms; she remains motionless and insensible to his tears, his caresses, to everything that he does. How much more touching this object is than the importunate wails and noisy regrets of her lover! He sees it, feels it, is torn by it. I have difficulty in dragging him off. If I leave him a moment, I shall never get him to leave. I am delighted that he carries with him this sad image. If ever he is tempted to forget what he owes to Sophie, and I recall her to his mind, as he saw her at the moment of his departure, his heart will have to be sadly alienated, if I cannot bring him back to her."

There may be differences of opinion in regard to the value of travelling at this juncture in a young man's life; but there can hardly be any in regard to the method by which Émile is induced, or rather forced, to undertake it. That a young man who, up

[1] Émile did, indeed, need to learn self-control.

to the age of twenty-two, has always followed, or thought he followed, his own inclination, should suddenly be commanded to set his strongest inclination at defiance, is a piece of the most wanton tyranny and cruelty, an attempt to reap where one has not sowed. That the young man, who does not know what obedience means, and who does not see his own interest or utility in what he is called upon to do, should obey, is not only extremely improbable, but very discreditable, showing that he has not escaped from the tyranny of his fellows, or become self-determining. He has taken a vow, like a mediæval monk, and is still subject to "obedience."[1] Still more improbable and discreditable is it that he should suddenly exchange his life-long, thoughtless, joyous optimism for a gloomy, disheartening, brooding pessimism, to which

> "The world is all a passing show,
> For man's illusion given."

But the worst feature of the whole matter is that, while calling upon his pupil to obey the voice of reason and conscience, Rousseau shows no reason why this voice should be obeyed, any more than the voice of passion and interest. So far as we are shown, both are equally subjective and blind, and there is no third faculty to be umpire between them. The moral law cannot remain a mere ungrounded "categorical imperative," but must be shown to be

[1] It is astonishing how many of the worst features of mediævalism — religious intolerance, mystic fanaticism, vows, confession, etc. — still survive in Rousseau. He had learnt much from the Jesuits.

the expression of man's essential relations to the universe. This, however, cannot be shown without a profound, painfully acquired, scientific knowledge of the world, and of man, as a coöperant, essentially social member of the same, nor without a carefully reasoned philosophy resting on this knowledge; and with these conditions, Rousseau, in his supercilious, unsocial subjectivism, claiming for itself supernatural inspiration, would have nothing to do.[1] It is not, therefore, wonderful that he landed in all sorts of contradictions, and, in the end, proved unfaithful to his own principles.

Émile leaves his Sophie, and sets out upon his travels, still accompanied by his despotic tutor. The purpose of these travels is ostensibly one of self-interest, — to enable Émile to discover the country in which he can settle down to quiet family life, with the best hope of independence and liberty. Rousseau holds that every man, when he comes to the age of discretion, has a right to choose his country. He tells us very little about Émile's travels; but he says many wise things regarding the value and method of travelling, as a means of education. Its value lies in the fact that it does away with local and national prejudices, puts experience in place of imagination, widens the sympathies, enables one to distinguish humanity under all guises, to reject what is accidental and spurious in it, and to cling to what is natural and

[1] Any one who claims a knowledge of theoretic or ethical principles, not grounded on experience, must be regarded as claiming inspiration. Even Kant, with his Rousselian "categorical imperative" was not exempt from this weakness.

genuine. Its method is that which brings the traveller most directly and closely in contact with the people of each country, enabling him to learn their language and become acquainted with their habits, customs, and ways of regarding things. The method of the ordinary tourist, whose main objects are scenery, cities, churches, galleries, museums, and public exhibitions, is altogether to be eschewed. Cities and city-people are pretty much the same all over Europe: they are all equally depraved by culture. "It is the country (*campagne*) that makes the country (*pays*), and the country people that make the nation." . . . "It is always in capitals that human blood is sold cheapest. Thus one becomes acquainted only with the great peoples, and the great peoples are all alike." . . . "The Europeans are no longer Gauls, Germans, Iberians, Allobroges; they are merely Scythians that have variously degenerated in face, and still more in morals." Émile, therefore, will merely glance at cities, and spend most of his time in remote country districts, where the people are still simple and undepraved. And he will not merely see and hear: he will also think. With his tutor he will discuss the origin and nature of social institutions, and of those relations and duties that arise under them. In this matter, little aid can be derived from books. "Political Right is a science which has yet to be born; and we may presume it never will be born. Grotius, the master of all our scholars in this matter, is but a baby, and, what is worse, a baby of bad faith. When I hear Grotius lauded to the skies, and Hobbes loaded with execrations, I see how much sensible men read or understand of these authors. The truth is, their principles are exactly similar; they differ only in expression. They differ also in method. Hobbes takes his stand on sophisms, Grotius on the poets; all the rest they have in common." . . . "The only modern man who might have created this great and useful science, was the famous Montesquieu. But he never thought of dealing with the principles of political right: he stopped short with the positive right of established governments; and no two things in the world are more different than these two studies." Such being the condition of things, Émile's tutor must help himself, as best he can, by means of original thinking.

It is but fair to say that the above criticisms of Hobbes, Grotius, and Montesquieu are, in the main, correct, and that to Rousseau himself is due a large share of the credit for originating the science of Political Right. With all its obvious mistakes, his *Social Contract* was an epoch-making book. We need not wonder, therefore, that the questions which Émile is led to consider are, in the main, those dealt with and answered in that book, or that he comes to the conclusions therein reached. Rousseau plainly admits this; and whatever we may think of these conclusions, we ought cheerfully to admit that hardly any book more provocative of thought — and such provocativeness is the greatest merit of any decent book — could be put into the hands of a young man of serious mind. If, while reading it, he have a wise and learned guide, he will see the extreme importance of the questions broached, and be led to inquiries and considerations which will reveal to him the fallacies involved in the attempt to answer them; and even if, for a short time, left to himself, he fall a victim to Rousseau's passionate and specious rhetoric, he will free himself as soon as the glamour of that has worn off, and through experience, study, and careful thought, seek other solutions of his own.[1]

After an absence of two years, devoted to experience and thought in social matters, Émile, who has all the time been looking out for a place to settle in, comes to the conclusion that one place (provided it is not in a city) is as good as another. "I remember," he says to his tutor, "that my property was the cause of our researches. You proved to me very cogently that I could not retain at once my riches and my liberty; but, when you wished me to be at once free and without needs, you were suggesting two things that are incompatible; for I cannot withdraw myself from dependence upon men, without reverting to dependence upon Nature. What, then, shall I do with my inherited fortune? I shall begin by ceasing to depend upon it; I shall slacken all the ties that bind me to it: if it is left to me, I shall keep it; if it is taken from me, I shall not be dragged off along with it. I shall not torment myself to retain it; but I shall

[1] The *Social Contract* ought to be a leading text-book in all classes in political science. It should be remembered that, in the hands of an able teacher, a bad book, calling for strong adverse criticism, is often far better than a good one, which leaves teacher and pupil nothing to do but to repeat and accept. Moreover, in these days, it is of no small importance that the false teaching of the *Social Contract*, still influential wherever there is not a profound acquaintance with political science, should be dragged to the light and exposed.

remain firm in my place. Rich or poor, I shall be free. I shall be so not only in such or such a country or region: I shall be so all the world over. For me all the chains of opinion are broken. I know only those of necessity. I have learnt to wear them since my childhood, and I shall wear them till the day of my death; for I am a man. And why should I not wear them in freedom, since I should still have to wear them in slavery, and those of slavery besides. What matters my position in the world? What matters it where I am? Wherever there are men, I am among my brothers: wherever there are none, I am at home with myself. As long as I can remain independent and rich, I have the means of living, and I shall live. When my property enslaves me, I shall abandon it without difficulty: I have arms to work with, and I shall live. When my arms fail me, I shall live, if I am supported; I shall die, if I am deserted. I shall die, even if I am not deserted; for death is not a punishment for poverty, but a law of Nature. Let death come when it will, I defy it: it will never find me making preparations to live: it will not prevent me from having lived. Such, father, is my fixed purpose. If I were without passions, I should, in my human condition, be independent as God himself, since, desiring only what is, I should never have to struggle with fate. At least, I shall have but one chain: it is the only one I shall always wear, and I may well be proud of it. Come, then, give me Sophie, and I am free."

Émile, having thus reached the desired mood of pessimistic, Stoic independence, and learnt to look upon life as a passing show, receives the commendations of his tutor, but is, at the same time, warned that he will not be quite so Stoical when he has children, and that he must submit to other yokes besides that of marriage. "O Émile!" says his tutor, "where is the good man that owes nothing to his country? Whoever he may be, he owes it man's most precious dower, the morality of his actions and the love of virtue. Born in the depths of a forest, he would have lived happier and freer; but, having nothing to resist in order to follow his passions, he would have been good without merit: he would not have been virtuous, whereas now he can be so in spite of his passions. The mere appearance of order prompts him to know and love it. The public good, which serves but as a pretext to others, is to him alone a real motive. He learns to battle with himself, to conquer himself, to sacrifice his own, to the common, interest. It is not true that he derives no benefit from the laws; they give him the courage to be just even among the wicked. It is not true that they have not made him free; they have taught him to rule himself."[1]

Émile is then shown that his place of abode ought not to be indifferent to him, and that "one of his duties is attachment to the place of his birth" and to his countrymen. "Live in the midst of them," exclaims the tutor; "cultivate their friendship in gentle intercourse; be their benefactor, their model. Your example will avail them more than all our books, and

[1] It is needless to remark that Rousseau here abandons the position toward civil life taken in the Discourses.

the good they see you do will touch them more deeply than all our vain talk. I do not advise you, on this account, to go and live in great cities; on the contrary, one of the examples which good men ought to set to others is to live a patriarchal, country life, the primitive life of man, the most peaceful, the most natural, and the sweetest for a man of uncorrupted heart." Following this advice, Émile resolves to take up his abode with Sophie's parents, and the long-desired marriage at last takes place, to the infinite joy of the lovers. When the ceremony is over, the tutor takes them aside, and, in a sensible, but ill-timed discourse, which makes the one protest and the other blush, shows them how they may indefinitely prolong their happiness, and remain lovers in the married state. He thereupon abdicates his authority, turning it over to Sophie.

When the honeymoon is over, the lovers settle down "to enjoy, in peace, the charms of their new condition." The tutor is happy over the results of his twenty-five years' labor. "How often," he says, "do I join their hands in mine, blessing Providence, and breathing ardent sighs! How many kisses do I pour upon these two hands that clasp each other! With how many tears of joy do they feel me water them! They, in turn, sharing my transports, melt with tenderness." At the end of some months Émile enters his tutor's room and, embracing him, informs him that he (Émile) will soon be a father. "But," he continues, "remain the master of the young masters. Advise us, govern us: we will be docile. As long as I live, I shall need you. I have more need of you than ever, now that my functions as a man are beginning. You have fulfilled yours; teach me to imitate you; and rest, for it is high time."

So, with the culmination of Émile's bliss, the book ends.

CHAPTER X

ROUSSEAU'S EDUCATIONAL THEORIES

MANHOOD

(*Émile and Sophie, or the Solitaries*)

> Dein eigen ist Alles,
> Dein Heil, wie dein Unheil,
> Dein Wollen und Wähnen,
> Dein Sinnen und Sein.
> JORDAN, *Die Nibelunge.*

> For man is man, and master of his fate.
> TENNYSON, *Idyls of the King.*

> Deus ipse voluntatem cogere non potest.
> THOMAS AQUINAS.

> There is no house prepared for thee after thy death, but that of which, before thy death, thou hast been the architect.
> AL GHAZZALI.

THERE can be little doubt that, when Rousseau finished *Émile* in 1762, he meant to end it, like other fairy tales, with "And so they were married, and lived happily ever after." In course of time, however, it seems to have struck him that an education which was good enough for well-mated, prosperous, and happy people, might be utterly useless for people otherwise situated. Accordingly in *Émile and Sophie, or the Solitaries*,[1] he undertook to show how his system

[1] This work, which was never finished, takes a form of a series of letters from Émile to his tutor. See p. 70.

would work in adversity. To do this, he had to break in upon the peaceful, patriarchal life of his wards, and to render both of them profoundly miserable, in fact, to drive them to the brink of despair.

After several years of undimmed happiness, during which a son and a daughter are born to them, Émile and Sophie are suddenly visited with a series of calamities, all the more terrible that the tutor has ceased to live with them. First, Sophie's father dies, then her mother, and, lastly, her idolized daughter. Untrained to misfortune, the poor young wife is utterly inconsolable, and fills the house and its surroundings with tears, sobs, and cries. In order to give her a needful change of environment, her husband, who now for the first time has "what is called business" in the capital, resolves to remove her thither, and take her to be near a friend whose acquaintance she has made in the neighborhood. Gloomy forebodings seize upon Émile as he approaches the city; but he shakes them off and proceeds. In the course of his two years' residence, amid the corrupting influences of city life, his whole being undergoes a change. Unguarded now by any tutor, and not subject to obedience, he forms new connections, acquires frivolous tastes, becomes a pleasure-seeker, and, though never unfaithful to his wife, finds his heart gradually losing all warmth and force. He becomes "gallant without tenderness, a Stoic without virtues, a sage given up to follies." At last he finds, or thinks he finds, that he no longer loves his wife. Meanwhile, his wife, as inexperienced as himself, and in need of distraction to lighten her

sorrow, allows herself to be drawn by her friend into
corrupt society, where she becomes familiarized, not
only with frivolity, but with vice, so that she gradually loses interest both in her husband and in her son.
Husband and wife, though still living under the same
roof, now become estranged from each other, and
lead separate lives. Finally, Sophie, under the influence of her corrupt, virtue-despising friend, and
apparently with but slight blame on her own part,
falls from virtue.[1] From this moment she avoids all
society, and sits lonely, gloomy, and tearful in her
own room. She expresses great horror of her friend
and her friend's husband, and Émile is obliged to
forbid them the house. Alarm at his wife's condition
now fans into a flame his smouldering affection, and
he tries to reëstablish the old intimate relations, but
finds her completely cold and irresponsive. His per-
sistent attentions, however, finally move her; but,
instead of deceiving him, as she might easily have
done, she heroically tells him: "I am no longer anything to you. . . . I am *enceinte*," darts into her room
and closes the door after her. Émile, completely
crushed and annihilated by this revelation, wanders
about for thirty-six hours, like a madman, without
sleep or food, devoured by the most poignant reflections and regrets. At last he reaches a village,
where he sups and sleeps soundly. The next day
he finds his way to a city, and enters the shop of a

[1] We are not permitted to know the details of this fall. "No,
never," writes Émile, "shall these hideous details escape my pen
or my mouth. It were too unjust to the memory of the worthiest of
women." . . . "Worldly morality, snare of vice and of example,
treason of false friendship, which of us is proof against you!"

carpenter, as an ordinary workman. Here he gradually comes to himself, realizes the nobility of his wife's declaration, and begins to feel that she may, after all, be far less culpable than he has thought. Unable to trust her, however, he resolves to remove his son from her keeping, and is making preparations to do this, when he learns that a lady with a child has come and, unseen, watched him at his work; that she has shown signs of great mental anguish; and that, after kneeling for a long time, she has risen and, pressing her cheek against that of the child, exclaimed in stifled tones: "No, he will never take your mother from you!" Émile at once recognizes the secret visitors to have been his wife and child, and is struck by his wife's sad words. They present to him a new aspect of the case. While he might be willing to remove the child from the guilty mother, he cannot think of removing the mother from the innocent child. So he resolves to do nothing in the matter. Having now, however, become an object of curiosity to his fellow-workmen and their wives, he resolves to avoid recognition and go further off in search of employment. He, accordingly, makes his way on foot to Marseilles, and takes passage on board a vessel bound for Naples, along with a number of other persons. The skipper proves to be a jolly, rollicking fellow, who does his best to keep his passengers in good humor; but Émile, who knows about the sun's course and about compasses, begins, after a time, to suspect that they are not going in the direction of their proposed destination. His suspicion is soon confirmed; for no sooner do they come in sight of land than they see a corsair coming toward them. Being without means of defence, they are soon boarded by the corsair's crew, whereupon it becomes evident that the skipper is in collusion with them, and that all the passengers, having been drawn into a trap, are destined to be the slaves of the Moors. The skipper does not long enjoy the success of his roguery; for Émile strikes off his head with a sabre, and sends it flying into the sea. By this act he earns the respect of his captors, and is not put in irons, like the rest of the passengers. On landing, however, he is sent, like the rest, to the galleys. Here, having time to reflect, he concludes that slavery, after all, is nothing so terrible. "Who can make me wear two chains?" he says. "Did I not wear one before? There is no real servitude but that to Nature; men are only its instruments. Whether a master finish me, or a rock crush me, the event is the same in my eyes, and the worst that can happen to me in slavery is not to be able to move a tyrant more than a stone. And, indeed, if I had my freedom, what should I do with it? In my present state, what can I desire? Alas! to prevent me from sinking into annihilation, I need to be animated with another's will in default of my own." This piece of characteristic Rousselian sophistry, which would justify any form of slavery, convinces him that his change of condition is more apparent than real, "that, if liberty consisted in doing what one wishes, no man would be free; that all are weak, dependent upon things and upon stern necessity; that he who can best will all that it ordains is the most free, since he is never forced to do what he does not wish."[1] And so, says Émile, "the days of my slavery were the days of my sovereignty, and I had never more authority over myself than when I was wearing the chains of the barbarians."

Émile comes into the possession of several masters, and is at first treated kindly, his owners hoping that friends will ransom him; but, as no efforts are made in his behalf, he is sent to work, and works cheerfully and well, while his companions, reared to be gentlemen and philosophers, and not to be men, only suffer and bewail their lot, many of them dying off from ill treatment. At last, Émile himself comes under a brutal overseer, who, observing him attempt to help his weaker comrades, so overloads him with work that he feels he must soon succumb under it. Seeing that, at the worst, he can only die, he foments a rebellion among his fellows, which the overseer vainly tries to lash down. This brings the owner upon the scene. Émile explains the facts to him, and appeals to his interest in such a way that the cruel overseer and Émile are made to exchange places. The latter proves an excellent overseer, and his conduct, getting noised abroad, comes to the ears of the Dey of Algiers, who desires to see him. This dey, a sensible man, who has worked his way up from the ranks, having taken a liking to him, receives him, as a gift, from his master. Thus, in every relation of life, even the most difficult and trying, Émile finds the value of

---

[1] Here we have the germs of the Schopenhauerian doctrine that true freedom consists in renouncing all will, even the "will to live," which means that to be happy is not to be at all — the last conclusion of pessimism.

his education, and its superiority to that of other men.

The work breaks off at this point; but its aim and outcome are obvious enough. The providential tutor, who has evidently foreseen everything, now goes to work to bring good out of evil. Thanks to the memory of a Genevese pastor, who was on friendly terms with Rousseau in his closing years, we know, in a general way, the close. "A succession of events brings Émile to a desert island. He finds on the shore a temple adorned with flowers and delicious fruits. He visits it every day, and every day he finds it decked out. Sophie is the priestess. Émile does not know this. What events can have brought her to these regions? The consequences of her fault and the actions which efface it. Sophie finally reveals herself. Émile learns the tissue of fraud and violence to which she has succumbed. But, unworthy henceforth to be his mate, she desires to be his slave and to serve her rival. This rival is a young person whom other events have joined to the lot of the former husband and wife. This rival marries Émile; Sophie is present at the wedding. Finally, after some days spent in the bitterness of repentance, and the torments of ever-renewed pain, all the more keen that Sophie makes it a duty and a point of honor to dissemble it, Émile and Sophie's rival confess that their marriage was only a make-believe. This pretended rival has a husband of her own, who is introduced to Sophie, and Sophie gets back her own, who not only forgives her involuntary fault, atoned for by the most cruel sufferings and redeemed by repentance, but values and honors, in her, virtues of which he had had but a faint notion, before they had found opportunity to unfold to their full extent."

Thus Rousseau has proved, to his satisfaction, two things: (1) that his education according to Nature will enable men and women to stand the test of the severest adversity, defying not only suffering, but also public opinion, and (2) that the life of cities is altogether corrupt and corrupting.

What becomes of Émile and Sophie, after their reconciliation, we are not told; but perhaps we may conclude that, finding themselves self-sufficient, they conclude to end their days, living after the fashion of Robinson Crusoe, or, rather, of Franz von Kleist's Zamori and his mate, on their desert island, thus returning to a state of Nature, whose charms are heightened by the bitter experiences of civilization.[1] It is just possible, however, that we have in the later books of *The New Héloïse* a picture of their conjugal happiness. Julie and Sophie have much in common, even their fall.

[1] See Emerson's poem, *The Adirondacks*.

CHAPTER XI

CONCLUSION.—ROUSSEAU'S INFLUENCE

The history of the world is the judgment of the world.
SCHILLER.

> Let him, the wiser man who springs
> Hereafter, up from childhood shape
> His action like the greater ape;
> But I was *born* for other things.
> TENNYSON, *In Memoriam*, CXX.

The history of mankind is a progress in the consciousness of freedom. HEGEL.

HAVING followed Rousseau's educational scheme from its beginning to its last effects upon manhood and womanhood, we have now to consider its value, to estimate its moral bearings, and to see whether it could properly lead to the results claimed for it.

That the influence of Rousseau's ideas upon educational theory and practice was, and is, great, no one will deny. In education, as in other things, his passionate rhetoric and his scorn for the conventional existent, as contrasted with the ideal simplicity of Nature, roused men from their slumbers, and made them reconsider all that they had so long blindly taken for granted and bowed before. And in so far his work was invaluable. His bitter, sneering condemnation of the corrupt, hypocritical, fashionable life of his time, with its distorting, debasing, and dehumanizing notions of education, and his eloquent plea for a return to a life truly and simply human, and to an education based upon the principles of human nature and calculated to prepare for such a life, were righteous and well timed. His purpose was thoroughly right, and he knew how to make himself heard in giving expression to it. But, when he came to inform the world in detail how this purpose was to be carried out, he undertook a task for which he was not fitted either by natural endowment or by education. His passionate, sensuous, dalliant, and immoral nature prevented him from seeing wherein man's highest being and aim consist, while his ignorance and his contempt for study, science, and philosophy closed his eyes to the historic process by which men have not only come to be what they now are, but by which their future course must be freely determined, and made him substitute for it a spurious scheme, put together out of certain vague notions of history afloat in his time and certain fancies of his own vivid imagination.

Thus, his own temperament and the reminiscences of his own capricious, undisciplined childhood led him to think that the child is a mere sensuous being, swayed by purely sensuous instincts, and inaccessible to reason or conscience, and that these, when called forth by social demands, are marks of depravation and badges of unfreedom. His utter inability to conceive of moral life, as a thoughtful adjustment of the individual to the universe, and as a self-sufficient end, for the attainment of which every sacrifice, intelligently and voluntarily made, is a gain, and ought to be a joy, made him, on the one hand, regard man as a mere plaything in the hands of a kindly but capricious God, and, on the other, to represent him as the helpless victim of an inexorable necessity or fate. Wavering hopelessly between these mutually contradictory Christian and Stoic notions, he never arrived at any conception of the true meaning of spiritual freedom, or the true ideal of social existence. His notion of freedom was almost purely negative, and, therefore, both empty and unsocial. He did not, and could not, see that freedom, like intelligence and affection, has no content save in a world wherein each individual spirit is, through its own essential ·activity, freely related to all other spirits, and gradually perfects itself by ever richer, deeper, and freer forms of this relation. He did not see that this process coincides with the gradual unfolding of reason and will, as they differentiate and particularize themselves out of that vague affection, or desiderant feeling, which constitutes the undeveloped soul. He did not see that even the first differentiation in the "fundamental feeling" involves consciousness and therefore reason, and the first movement in obedience to one feeling, rather than another, the first stirring of selective conscience, or will. He did not see that the gradual differentiation of feeling into perceptions and volitions is the gradual creation of a world of beings in thought and will, that things and persons are distinguished through an effort to group feelings and satisfactions, by referring them to particular common sources, and that, apart from this process, there would be no consciousness, and no world, at all. In a word, he failed altogether to see that existence is essentially social and, therefore, moral, alien alike to caprice and to necessity. As a consequence of this, he failed to understand the true nature of education, which is simply the effort to enable children, from the moment they begin to use reason and will, that is, to distinguish one feeling and one attraction from another, so to classify and group these feelings and attractions that an orderly, self-consistent, and rational world, with a hierarchy of well-defined attractions, shall gradually shape itself in their minds, and make a rational and moral life possible for them. In denying reason and conscience to the child, he was denying it the very agencies by which its world is built up, and, in trying to isolate it from society, he was depriving it of a large portion, and that too the most important, of those feelings or experiences with which these agencies have to work, and so impoverishing the child's world. The truth is, Rousseau himself had no rationally or morally organized world of his own. Much remained for him in the condition of almost brute feeling or emotion, round which his fancy played in the most capricious fashion. Then, when he attempted arbitrarily to introduce unity into this chaotic world, he invented for the purpose, out of old traditions, sometimes a capricious, and sometimes a necessary, first principle, neither of which could, in the nature of things, organize that world, or give him any real freedom in it. A mind like his, incapable of reducing its world to clear visibility and transparent unity, was naturally dependent upon its unorganized moods, and was liable to pass from the most joyous optimism, at one leap, to the gloomiest pessimism. This is the secret of his emotional deism, of his sudden change from Epicureanism to Stoicism, from spontaneity to authority in Émile's education, and of his oscillation between religious intolerance and the most complete liberalism.[1]

The failure of Rousseau to realize that education is the process by which a world of rational distinctions and ends is developed in the child's mind, also closed his eyes to the fact that it must be so conducted that the distinctions made by the child form, as far as possible, a coherent, self-explaining whole at every moment, and that this whole shall be duly articulated as fast as it grows, leaving no undigested clots of feeling or experience to baffle and stupefy the expanding mind. As a result of this, his educational system, though divided into epochs, is otherwise altogether disorderly, and he is far more interested that the child should enjoy himself, revelling in a present chaos of disconnected sensations, than that he should know the joy of creating for himself, out of them, a rational and eternal world. Hence his frivolous and oft-repeated plea that the future should be sacrificed to the present, for fear that the future may never come — a strange enough caution for one who pretended to believe in immortality. If that is a fact, then surely all spiritual gains made by the human being, at any

---

[1] See above, p. 184. In *The New Héloïse*, Pt. III., Let. V., he says: "No true believer can be intolerant or a persecutor. If I were a magistrate, and the law ordained the burning of atheists, I should begin by burning, as such, the first man who informed against another."

period of his life, will tell to all eternity, no matter when he leaves this earthly scene; and he can do nothing more recklessly foolish than forget the future in the present. But, in making this plea, Rousseau, characteristically enough, failed altogether to see that, even for a child, there is a much higher sort of enjoyment than mere capricious, sensuous dalliance, namely, the enjoyment that comes from an orderly exertion of his will in view of an end, and was utterly unaware that such exertion is the process by which all strong and consistent characters are formed. We need not, therefore, be surprised to find Émile arriving at the age of twenty, so destitute of all ends and aims that, if he were not watched at every moment, night and day, he would become an easy prey to his dalliant sensibilities. A young man who has learnt to make the present subservient to the future by the exercise of his will, in the continual pursuit of worthy ends, and who knows the delight that comes from the attainment of these, will hardly be so victimized.

It may perhaps be permitted to point out here that the great educational principle of introducing unity and system into life, by completing the present with the future, is embodied in the beautiful Praxitelean group of Hermes and the Infant Dionysus. Here we have the ideal tutor and pupil. The elder god, the perfect type of glorious young manhood, carries the younger, a highly intelligent, almost mature-faced child, on his left arm. The child places his right hand on the shoulder of his guardian, stretches his left out toward something, probably a bunch of grapes, which the latter holds aloft in his left, and looks beseechingly into his face. But Hermes does not return the look, or smile. His earnest eyes have a far look. In tempting forth into action the child's natural desires, he is gazing, not at the present, but at the distant future. This expresses the spirit of Greek education, whose patron Hermes was, as well as of all education whose purpose is to make strong, wise, determined men.

A very striking result of Rousseau's sensuous nature was his view of women, and of the education proper for them. For him, woman is never a spiritual being, the equal of man in freedom, an end to herself, and entering into sexual relations by free choice for certain ends, by her desired and approved. She is merely a female, the slave and instrument of man, a creature whose whole being is exhausted in her sexuality. Her education, therefore, is merely the education of her sexuality, and ought, on no account, to go beyond this. Rousseau's conception of women is one that has been only too common in France, as in all countries where the Moslem pseudo-virtue of chivalry, or external palaver in their presence, has taken the place of that real virtue of inner gentlemanliness, which regards women first as human beings, endowed with all human attributes and rights, and afterwards as women, with special duties and privileges. It is a conception which, while pretending to elevate women into mistresses, degrades them into slaves, and deprives them of that dignity of freedom, which alone imparts value to life.

If Rousseau's character led him into manifold errors, his contemptuous ignorance of philosophy, science, and history led him into many more. Thus, in addition to assuming a relation of opposition between sensation and reason, and thereby introducing a Manichæan division into the individual man, he placed a similar opposition between Nature and Culture, and thereby broke the continuity, and rendered unintelligible the course, of social evolution. Worse than this, having failed to recognize that all existence is essentially social and moral, and regarding the unsocial, sub-moral man as complete and self-sufficient, he was bold enough to maintain that all social relations and all the powers, intellectual and moral, demanded and evolved by these, are so many forms of degeneration. Believing that man was forced into sociability only by selfish motives, and that society exists only to enable him to preserve as much as possible of his natural Cyclopean [1] freedom,[2] he continually holds up the state of Nature, in which man is a mere instinct-guided animal, living wholly in the present, without plan or purpose, as his ideal condition, to be regained whenever possible. His whole system of education, accordingly, aims at rendering men unsocial, and so might fitly enough be called Unsocial Education. We need not, therefore, be surprised that Émile never develops any social virtues other than those of the family and the kindly neighbor, never engages in any social, economic, or political reforms, and never looks upon social duties except as obtruding evils that, in a culture-perverted life, must be borne with Stoic indifference or resignation.

[1] See Homer, *Odyssey*, Bk. IX., 112 sqq.
[2] He has rare glimpses of a better view; but they do not last. See p. 200.

If, owing to his defective character and acquirements, Rousseau's educational system is mainly false in presuppositions and aims, it is still more so in method. To train a being whose nature is essentially moral, and whose life, in so far as moral, must consist in relations and dealings with free, intelligent beings, by the laws of brute necessity and force, with the view of imparting to him the freedom of an automaton, is surely the height of absurdity, and the author of another volume in this series is entirely justified in calling the attempt "a scheme as fantastic as ever entered the wayward mind of a madman — to separate the child from his fellows, and set him in a wilderness."[1] This scheme had its origin, partly in Rousseau's character, which was essentially unsocial and impatient of moral regulation, and partly in his false notions of the origin and uses of society. To be sure, if one does not care to learn to swim, he need not go into the water; but if he does wish, he has no choice. So, if we wish a child to make his way safely in society, we must bring him up in society, familiarize him with its laws, usages, and meaning, and train his will to relate itself freely to the freedom of other wills. To make brute force the sole means of his education is to dehumanize him, to make him an outcast from the hour of his birth. If, in spite of such treatment, his human nature still asserts itself, it will be in an altogether undeveloped form. The child will be a dependent cry-baby and stupid dupe at the age of sixteen, and as such, indeed, Émile is presented to us. Moreover, since utter subjection to the control

[1] Bowen, *Froebel*, p. 4.

of necessity cuts off all possibility of control by self, and leaves the child entirely determined from without, he will have to be watched and tended all the days of his life, and, in case of need, subjected to unblushing tyranny, as we find Émile to have been. He never learns to distinguish between slavery and freedom, for the simple reason that he never has any experience of the latter. When one cannot tell slavery from freedom, there is no heroism in bearing it,[1] and no motive to throw it off. Men with Émile's principles would accept slavery and oppression with Stoic indifference, or else revert to savagery; and the struggle for concrete freedom, that is, freedom with a content of social relations, as distinct from negative freedom without relations, would come to an end.

But, besides all these defects of presuppositions, ideals, and method inherent in Rousseau's system, it is chargeable with three others which are fatal: (1) it is exclusive, (2) it is impracticable, and (3) it is immoral.

In the world for which Rousseau, however inconsistently, paved the way, all education must be universal, accessible to every human being, as such, without distinction of class or sex. Now, Rousseau's system

---

[1] To regard indiscriminating apathy as moral heroism, or to look for peace through the blunting of sensibilities, is the height of absurdity. Cf. *Macbeth*, IV., 3:

Malcolm. Dispute it like a man.
Macduff. I shall do so;
　　But I must also feel as a man.

This is the true heroism, and the only one that is compatible with social life or individual nobility. It is a chief task of education to cultivate keenness of feeling.

never laid claim to any such universality. He maintains that the poor have no need of education (see p. 106 n.), and considers only the rich and well born. His system is, therefore, essentially exclusive, aristocratic, and plutocratic, an education for kindly country squires, or rural patriarchs, living in the midst of thralls or serfs. But, even as exclusive, it is utterly impracticable. It would be impossible to find a man willing to devote the twenty-five best years of his life, without reward, to the education of one child, even if that child were his own; and, if he could be found, his self-sacrifice, and his renunciation of all social relations and duties, for the sake of one who might not live, or might not develop, to justify his efforts, would be an insane act. The world would not make much progress, if every child required the exclusive services of a tutor for five and twenty years, and, even at the end of that time, had not learnt to guide his own life. Again, unless desert islands could be produced at will, the isolation demanded by the system is impossible. Indeed, we do not find that Rousseau can dispense with society. His Émile attends fairs, ice-cream parties, and banquets, and runs races for cakes with other children; and such experiences are shown to be necessary parts of his education. In all this, Rousseau forgot himself. Lastly, a system which uses, as its sole motive, self-interest, and that too, frequently in low forms; which estimates actions by their actual, instead of their intended, consequences, and which continually practises pious fraud and dupery, in order to reach its ends, surely deserves to be called immoral. And its acknowledged result upon Émile, who never rises to the dignity of a rational, self-determining personality, freely relating himself to a society of free personalities, but always remains the victim of a sensuous, capricious, selfish Epicureanism, dashed with fitful blotches of gloomy, fatalistic, despairing Stoicism, crying, like a spoilt child, at one moment, and posing as a Prometheus Bound the next, fully bears out this judgment.

Gathering up, in one glance, the various defects of Rousseau's social and pedagogical theories, we can now see clearly the false assumption that lay at the bottom of them all. It is a very common and widespread error, and is fatal wherever it occurs. It consists in assuming that the later and higher stages in evolution are to be explained by the laws that manifest themselves in the earlier and lower, and must be made to square with these. It throws forward the darkness of the earlier upon the later, instead of casting back the light of the later upon the earlier. Thus it continually tries to explain human nature by the laws manifested in sub-human nature, and insists that man should go back and allow himself to be governed by the necessary[1] laws of the latter, — ὁμολογουμένως τῇ φύσει, as the fatalistic Stoics said. This is the sum and substance of Rousseau's teaching in sociology, ethics, and pedagogy; it is the sum and substance of much popular teaching in all departments of theory and practice to this day. And yet nothing

---

[1] It is hardly necessary to say, in these days, that the notion of necessity corresponds to no fact that we know. Nature reveals regularity, but not necessity. See Huxley, *Materialism and Idealism*, in *Collected Essays*, Vol. I.

could be more misleading, more fatal to progress. The acorn does not explain the oak, but the oak the acorn. The *meaning* of the acorn is revealed in the oak, and the meaning of Nature in Culture. "Nature," Professor James tells us, "reveals no spiritual intent." Of course it does not, so long as you arbitrarily exclude from Nature its highest manifestations; but include these, and you will see that they are what all Nature has been tending toward from all eternity. In a word, Culture is the meaning, or intent, of Nature, and we shall never know the full meaning of the first and lowest step in existence till the last and highest has been taken. Each to-day reveals the meaning of all yesterdays, and contains the free promise of all to-morrows. The problem of life is, not to make man live according to Nature, but to make Nature live according to man, or, in less ambitious phrase, to elevate the "natural" into the "spiritual" man, blind instinct into rational freedom. Rousseau's system, therefore, exactly inverts the order of Nature and progress; it advocates the descent, not the ascent, of man.[1]

To sum up: In so far as Rousseau laid bare the defects and abuses of the society and education of his time, and demanded reforms in the direction of truth and simplicity, he did excellent work; but, when he came to tell how such reforms were to be accomplished, he propounded a system which, from a social

[1] Aristotle, who never falls into the common error, calls the oak, as the meaning of the acorn, the what-it-was-ness ($\tau\grave{o}\ \tau\acute{\iota}\ \mathring{\eta}\nu\ \epsilon\tilde{\iota}\nu\alpha\iota$) of it. We say of the acorn, when we see the oak that has sprung from it, "Oh, that's what it was!" The republic of free spirits is the what-it-was-ness of the lowest form of life.

and moral point of view, has hardly one redeeming feature, and which is frequently in glaring contradiction with itself. It is pure Romanticism.

In spite of this, it has been given to few men to exert, with their thought, an influence so deep and pervasive as that of Rousseau. This influence, due to the fact that he took the "motions" which were "toiling in the gloom" of the popular mind of his time, and made them flash, with the lurid lightning of his own passion, before the eyes of an astonished world, extended to all departments of human activity — philosophy, science, religion, art, politics, ethics, economics, and pedagogy.

In Philosophy this influence is very marked. Kant has told us that he was "roused from his dogmatic slumber" by Hume, and this is true; but, after he was roused, he drew his chief inspiration from Rousseau.[1] The germinal thought of the *Critique of the Pure Reason*, expressed in its opening sentence, is to be found in *Émile*, Bk. IV.[2] "These comparative ideas, *greater*, *less*, as well as the numerical ideas, *one*, *two*, etc, are certainly not sensations, though the mind produces them only on the occasion of sensations" — the Critical Philosophy is but a generalization of this. We have already seen that Kant's three "Postulates of the Pure Reason" — God, Freedom, and Immortality [3] — are simply Rousseau's three fun-

[1] He is said never to have omitted his afternoon walk but once, and that was when he got absorbed in *The New Héloïse*. It is difficult to understand this nowadays.
[2] Savoyard Vicar's *Confession of Faith*.
[3] See p. 166, and cf. Prologue to Tennyson's *In Memoriam*.

damental tenets of natural religion. Kant's ethical rigorism, with its ungrounded "categorical imperative," owes much to Rousseau's spasmodic Stoicism; while his theory of taste, as laid down in his *Critique of the Power of Judgment,* clearly has its roots in Rousseau's definition of taste.[1] It is hardly an exaggeration, therefore, to say that Kant, in his three Critiques, does little more than present, in philosophic garb, the leading doctrines of Rousseau. But, as has already been shown, Rousseau had occasional glimpses of truth that lay altogether beyond Kant's range of vision.[2] Through Kant, Rousseau's philosophic influence passed into all German, and thence into all modern, philosophy, as could easily be shown. Even the latest developments, Agnosticism and Philopistism,[3] can be traced back, through Kant's unknowable "thing-in-itself," and undemonstrable "postulates," to Rousseau's emotional subjectivism. The result of Rousseau's influence upon philosophy has been to discredit human reason, to replace it by infectious emotion, and to pave the way for a return to obscurantism and superstition.[4]

[1] See p. 175.   [2] See above, p. 85, note.

[3] I cannot think of any better compound to express the irrational "will-to-believe"-ism of such recent writers as Drummond, Balfour, Kidd, and James. See Cecil's *Pseudo-Philosophy at the End of the Nineteenth Century.* It is needless to say that Agnosticism and Philopistism are respectively but the emotionally pessimistic and optimistic aspects of one fact, the despair, on the part of reason, of solving its own problems — a despair originally born of Rousseau's intellectual sloth.

[4] See the quotation from Gœthe, on p. 113. Gœthe, as we shall see, overcame the influence of Rousseau. He puts many of his teachings, almost *verbatim,* into the mouth of Mephistopheles, and of Faust in his dark days.

The same thing is true of his influence upon Science, although this, thanks to the fact that science, wiser than philosophy, takes due account of the sensuous content of thought, has been less marked. The results of science are proof against emotional prejudice, and take no notice of contempt. It was specially to Hegel and his school that this part of Rousseau's influence passed. Hegel spoke with undisguised contempt of physical science, and constructed philosophies of religion, right, art, etc., out of his own brain — philosophies which science has silently converted into warning examples. His thought has almost been forgotten in the land of its birth, and many of his works have never had the honor of a second edition.

In Religion, Rousseau's influence has been incalculable, supplementing, and, in some ways, counteracting, that of Voltaire. While Voltaire and his followers were applying a robust, but rather coarse, common sense to the ancient word-castles of religious dogma, and reducing them to heaps of crumbling ruins, Rousseau was trying to construct a simple cottage out of a few moth-eaten sticks rescued from the general wreck, by covering over with a thin papering of varnished sentiment. The result was the Savoyard Vicar's *Confession of Faith*, a frail enough structure, not fit for human habitation, save in the mildest weather. It, nevertheless, proved widely attractive at a time when men, having lost faith, not only in religion, but also in reason, as interpreters of life, were fain to look to sentiment and romance for help. Rousseau's emotional faith became the religion of many men in his own time, of a large party among the French revolutionists, — Robespierre, St. Just, etc., — and of millions of pious but uncritical souls afterwards. It contributed important elements to the Neo-Catholic renaissance in the Latin countries, and to the Protestant reaction in the Germanic, as well as to English and American Unitarianism. It is the determining element in the extensive theological movements initiated by Schleiermacher and Ritschl, and is perpetuated in thousands of learned books down to our own time, when it forms the chief element in religion, taking the place of dogma, and so bidding defiance to the results of criticism, "higher" and lower. Thanks, in great part, to Rousseau, religion has, in our time, become a matter, not of spiritual insight and settled conviction, which in their nature are universal, but rather of sentiment and emotion, which are necessarily individual. It was a great misfortune for France, as well as for the world, that, when changes in life and developments in science made a new attitude in regard to religion necessary, the matter should have fallen into the hands of two such men as Voltaire and Rousseau, who, being equally without profound knowledge, philosophical acumen, and moral firmness, were utterly unfitted to deal worthily with it. The one pulled down with the tools of scornful wit and insidious persiflage; the other built up with the nervous, ineffective hands of romantic sentiment and dalliant emotion. The result has been, on the one hand, an irrational, paralyzing scepticism, and, on the other, an enfeebling, voluptuous mysticism, both equally favorable to superstition and to neglect of moral life. Between these France has been suffering **depletion and exhaustion** for over a hundred years.

In Art, and especially in Literature, Rousseau's influence has, from his own days to ours, been almost paramount throughout Christendom. Indeed, modern art and literature, with their fondness for the picturesque, the natural, the rural, the emotionally religious, the analysis of sentiment, and the interplay of passions, and their rebellion against the stiff and the conventional, may almost be said to date from Rousseau. There is no room here to trace his footsteps in the studiedly rural cottages and picturesque, half-wild parks, so common in Europe and America; in the landscape paintings, genre-pictures, and pictures of pathetic or religious emotion, that fill our galleries; or in the nature groups and sentimentally posed figures that delight the majority of our sculptors; but we must follow them here and there in the paths of literature, on which they are everywhere to be found, in France, in Germany, in England, in Italy, in Greece, in Scandinavia, in Russia. As to French literature, in the last hundred years, it is soaked in Rousseau's teaching from beginning to end. Its form and its matter are alike due to him. Its simplicity, its clear and effective style, its frequent glittering superficiality, its morbid pathos and insincere virtue, its outspokenness and lubricity are among its debts to him. Bernardin de St. Pierre and Madame de Staël; Lamartine and De Vigny; Châteaubriand and Montalembert; Saintaine and De Maistre; Mérimée and Michelet; De Musset and George Sand; Victor Hugo and Balzac; Dumas and Eugène Sue; Souvestre and De Senancour; Cousin and Renan; Taine and Ste. Beuve; Bourget and Zola; Coppée and Loti; Gautier and Amiel, with hundreds more, are all his disciples. He is the parent alike of the Neo-Christians and the decadents; of the romanticists and the realists. It may be added that his influence has been far greater than Voltaire's.

When we turn to German literature, we find almost the same condition of things. The Storm-and-Stress Period in Germany was mainly due to the ferment caused by Rousseau's teaching. It affected her greatest geniuses, Gœthe and Schiller, Kœrner and Von Kleist. Gœthe, at first, completely succumbed to it, as we see from such works as the *Triumph of Sentimentality* and the *Sorrows of Young Werther;* but his strong nature in time threw it off, and turned to a healthy classicism. Nevertheless, its traces appear in all his works, especially in his lyrics, many of which Rousseau, had he been an artist, might have written. And, after all, Faust is only a grown-up Émile, breaking away from faith and culture, and entrusting himself to a bad tutor; while Wilhelm Meister is an Émile with no tutor at all. Schiller was still more deeply and permanently influenced. His lyrics are full of Rousselian "Nature," pathos, and emotional religiosity, while his *Robbers*, that chaotic drama of wild revolt, might have been written by Rousseau. Indeed, Rousseau's lachrymose sentimentality and emotional prodigality seized upon the German people, like an epidemic, and long affected, for the most part injuriously, both its life and its literature. We can trace them in Kœrner and Kotzebue; in the Von Kleists and Schlegels; in the Humboldts and Grimms; in Fichte and Schelling; in Novalis and Richter; in Heine and Rueckert; in Lenau and Platen; in Freytag and Auerbach; in Heyse and Spielhagen; in Fanny Lewald and Johanna Ambrosius, and in many more.

In England, Rousseau's influence upon literature, though all-pervasive, was, in the main, beneficial. The English bee sucked the honey and rejected the poison, for the most part, only becoming occasionally dizzy with the opium of nature-mysticism. Under the influence of Rousseau, the poets of Great Britain broke away from the monotonous, aphoristic stiltedness of Pope and his school, and returned to "Nature" and simplicity. Burns, whose debt to Rousseau was very great, and Lady Nairne led the way. They were followed by Keats,[1] Shelley, and Byron; Southey, Coleridge, and Wordsworth;[2] Leigh Hunt and the

---

[1] Keats came nearer to Rousseau, in intensity of feeling for Nature, than any other man, and he was of finer texture.

[2] Wordsworth, "that uttered nothing base," was, in all but moral infirmity, a thorough-going disciple of Rousseau. He even followed him in his mystic feeling for Nature, and his confusion of the tenderly emotional with the ethical. Hence such sheer nonsense as this:—

> "One impulse from a vernal wood
> May teach you more of man,
> Of moral evil and of good,
> Than all the sages can."

If this be true, let us abandon all sages and all books, and sit at the feet of some "vernal wood"! Wordsworth is full of such beguiling untruths. What, for example, could be more untrue than that "the child is father of the man," or that "our birth is but a sleep and a forgetting"? His whole emotional pantheism, so dear to sensuous dalliers, is Rousselian and immoral to the core.

Brownings; Carlyle and Ruskin;[1] Clough and Tennyson; Morris and Swinburne; Dickens and Thackeray; George Eliot and Mrs. Ward. On the other side of the Atlantic, they were followed by Longfellow and Lowell; Whittier and Emerson. Apart from American differences, the last is the most loyal disciple that Rousseau ever had. His patriarchal country life came as near as possible to Rousseau's highest ideal. And their whole view of the world, and of their relations to it, were very much the same. Both loved Nature, and felt inexpressible mystic meanings in it; both preferred solitude, and felt that society was in conspiracy against the freedom of the individual; both were pantheists and, in theory, Stoics. Emerson's essay on *Self-reliance* would have delighted Rousseau. Both avoided social ties and political life. Both believed that man is essentially good, and will develop best, if left to give free expression to his spontaneity. Both believed in an Oversoul, of which man is merely a partaker, and to which he ought to lay himself open in passive receptivity. Both scorned consistency, and sought to draw the most from each passing mood. Both were averse to consecutive, logical thought and sustained scientific inquiry. And the list of resemblances might be added to indefinitely. But Emerson was a Puritan.

Italian literature did not escape the universal contagion. The writings of Leopardi and Foscolo; Manzoni and D'Azeglio; Carducci and Costanzo; Rapisardi

[1] The resemblance of these two men, in different ways, to Rousseau is very remarkable. The one inherited his contempt for civilization, the other his love of Nature.

and D'Annunzio, not to mention Ada Negri and many others, are all more or less inspired by Rousseau. There is no room to speak of the literatures of Greece, Scandinavia, and Russia; but what is true of the others is equally true of them. Ibsen, for example, is Rousselian to the core, in his contempt for society and its hollow, soul-corrupting conventions.

It is almost superfluous to speak of Rousseau's influence on Politics, practical and theoretical. He is the father of Democracy. The French Revolution was, in very large degree, his work. While repressive respect for authority in life and thought was relinquishing its hold, under the inexorable lash of Voltaire's bitter tongue, Rousseau was passionately calling upon the men, thus set free, to rise up, cast off their loosened chains, and claim the freedom with which God and Nature had endowed them, and live thenceforth in "Liberty, Equality, and Fraternity." His passion prevailed, and France rose in blind fury, bathed herself in blood, and lighted a conflagration that burnt for thirty years. When, at last, it was quenched in blood, Europe hardly recognized herself. She looked the same; but she felt that she was not the same. Authority, in the old sense, had been burnt away, and a green crop of freedom was springing up in its place. What this meant, neither France nor the other nations of Europe have yet learnt; but they are learning. And they are learning also that most important of all social lessons, that no revolution, inspired by such irreverent and passionate motives as those furnished by Voltaire and Rousseau, can fail to bring destruction and woe, which only the gentle, slow-moving hand of Reason can wipe away.

If the American Revolution was due to the spirit of liberty inherent in the English people, the formulas in which the Declaration of Independence was couched were largely drawn from Rousseau. When its framers demanded "life, liberty, and the pursuit of happiness" for every citizen, they were speaking in his language. Their calmer natures, formed for political freedom, enabled them to avoid his sentimental exaggerations, and to make provision for it; but his influence helped to make them forget that every Declaration of Independence needs to be supplemental by a Declaration of Interdependence. As a result, we are too fond of political isolation, and too prone to individual isolation. As a people, we are slow to recognize our duties to other peoples; as individuals, we are sadly deficient in public spirit, and in loyalty to what our constitution stands for. The hand of the unsocial Rousseau is still heavy upon us, carrying us back to savagery.

Upon Political Theory the effect of Rousseau's teaching has been so great that he may fairly be called the father of modern political science. Though that science, in its progress, has shown most of his positions to be baseless, it is none the less true that these have formed the centre of all political speculation for the last hundred years. He gave wrong answers to the questions which he propounded; but these questions were just the ones that required to be answered. The Social Contract does not lie at the beginning of social progress, but is the end to which it forever tends.

Hovering between two equally immoral systems,

Epicureanism and Stoicism, and having apparently no experience of free will, Rousseau developed no Ethical System. Nevertheless, his views were not without effect upon subsequent ethical theories. His notion that we have a sense for good, just as we have a sense for smell, — a notion which takes morality out of the region of reason and will altogether, — has found many followers among sentimentalists; while his doctrine that man should not seek to rise above the laws of necessity,[1] but remain an automaton, has found favor with all those who have sought to interpret Culture by Nature, instead of Nature by Culture. His insidious glorification of sensuous dalliance has, naturally, found a response in all dalliant natures.

In the sphere of Economics, Rousseau's influence, though great, is quite different from what he expected. Though entirely averse to socialism and anarchism, he was in large degree the parent of both. They arose from the spirit of his teaching, rather than from his teaching itself. In his remarkable article on *Political Economy*, written for the *Encyclopédie*, he points out the danger of looking upon society as an organism, most strongly defends the rights of private property, and justifies the State in imposing taxes. "It is certain," he says, "that the right of property is the most sacred of all the rights of the citizens, more important in certain aspects than liberty itself, whether because it is more closely connected with the preservation of life, or because property, being more easy to usurp, and more difficult to defend, than person, ought to be more carefully respected, or, finally,

[1] Cf. *Faust*, Prologue in Heaven, lines 39-50.

because property is the true foundation of civil life, and the true warrant for the obligations of citizens; for, if property were not responsible for persons, nothing would be so easy as to elude one's duties and defy the laws." . . . "The first thing which the founder of a commonwealth has to do, after laying down laws, is to find a fund sufficient for the support of magistrates and other officers, and for all public expenses. This fund is called *œrarium* or *fisc*, if it is in money; public domain, if it is in land; and for obvious reasons, the latter is far preferable to the former." . . . "A public domain is the surest and most honest of all means of providing for the needs of the state." Though holding this, he does not object to taxation, merely insisting that it shall not be imposed except by a vote of the people. But, when he inveighs, with bitter scorn, against the venality and corruption of public officials, and maintains that "it is one of the most important functions of government to prevent extreme inequalities of fortune, not by taking accumulated wealth away from its possessors, but by depriving them of the means to accumulate it; and not by building hospitals for the poor, but by guaranteeing citizens against the chance of becoming such," he accepts the fundamental principle of socialism, which naturally calls forth its opposite, anarchism; and principles have a vitality far beyond the will and intent of him who propounds them. Moreover, Rousseau's Stoicism is virtual socialism, while his Epicureanism is virtual anarchism, as could easily be shown. It ought to be added that one of the noblest and most conspicuous traits in Rousseau's character was unfailing sympathy with the poor and oppressed, involving hatred of their oppressors; and it is this sympathy and this hatred, which his example did much to make common, that have, respectively, caused the socialistic and anarchistic movements of this century.

Finally, in Education, the influence of Rousseau has been powerful beyond measure. He may fairly be called the father of modern pedagogy, even despite the fact that most of his positive teachings have had to be rejected. Comenius, Locke, and others had, indeed, done good work before him; but it was he that first, with his fiery rhetoric, made the subject of education a burning question, and rendered clear its connection with all human welfare. The whole gospel of modern education lies in such passages as this: "It is from the first moment of our lives that we ought to learn to deserve to live; and as, at our birth, we share in the rights of citizens, the moment of our birth ought to be the beginning of the exercise of our rights. If there are laws for man's estate, there ought to be laws for children, teaching them to obey others;[1] and, seeing that we do not leave each man's private reason to be sole judge of his duties, we ought to be all the more reluctant to hand over to the notions and prejudices of fathers the education of their children, that it affects the State more than it does them." It would have been well had Rousseau clung firmly to these ideas.

Of Rousseau's educational demands, perhaps only

[1] It is needless to note that this teaching is utterly at variance with that advanced in *Émile*.

three have been responded to: (1) the demand that children should, from the moment of their birth, be allowed complete freedom of movement; (2) that they should be educated through direct experience, and not through mere information derived from books; (3) that they should be taught to use their hands in the production of useful articles. But certain others of his notions lingered on for a time, much to the detriment of education, and were with difficulty shaken off. It is needless to say that his doctrines influenced all subsequent educators.

Among these the first important and influential name is that of his countryman Pestalozzi. This genial saint undertook to reduce to practice what Rousseau had preached, and even went so far as to isolate his own son for that purpose. Having discovered the folly of this and, therewith, the futility of Rousseau's exclusive education, and being moved with pity for the condition of the laboring classes, sunk in helpless ignorance, he set about evolving a plan whereby this ignorance might be removed and the poor rendered self-helpful. Thus his sympathy for the common people led him to a course altogether different from that recommended by Rousseau, who held that the poor required no education. The truth was, that, though Pestalozzi started from the same point as Rousseau, their ideas of education were diametrically opposed. Rousseau regarded education merely as a means of protecting its subjects from the corruptions of civilization, and securing for them as much as possible of their natural liberty, whereas Pestalozzi looked upon it as a means of enabling men to live a social and moral life. But, as has often been said, Pestalozzi was a sentimental philanthropist, rather than a philosophic educator. He was more anxious that his pupils should learn to make an honest living than that they should be harmoniously developed spiritual beings, and hence he directed his chief efforts to the former end. He responded to Rousseau's three demands, and followed him in his emotional religiosity; but he developed no educational principles or methods, based upon the nature and ends of the child. His crowning merit lay in seeing that nothing can help the people but education, and in demanding that this should be made universal. His example, too, inspired others to do what he could not. Among these others, the most notable and effective were Herbart (1776–1841) and Frœbel (1782–1852).

Herbart, a philosopher who, having revolted from the formalism of Kant, had betaken himself to the study of psychology, was, apparently, just the man to supply what Pestalozzi had omitted, and, indeed, in his own way, he did so. Setting out with a metaphysical, somewhat Leibnizian, conception of the soul, as a monad, he tried to show by what process, in its endeavor to preserve its existence against other monads, continually impinging upon it and invading it, it gradually, through successive "apperceptions," built up that complex of ideas which made its world rational, and enabled it to lead a moral life. Such life, in active relation with sub-human nature and with society, he conceived to be the end of all education. In this he was undoubtedly right, and his system may almost be said to be diametrically opposed to that of Rousseau. Unfortunately, his academic formalism and want of experience betrayed him into a metaphysic that was purely fanciful, having no foundation either in dialectic or in experience, and into a psychology that was to the last degree mathematical, materialistic, and mechanical. Ideas are treated as forces which may be compounded, and whose mechanical relations and resultants may be stated in mathematical formulas. With such notions he could, of course, arrive at no conception of a free will or any true morality.[1] To him will is nothing more than the mechanical resultant of his idea-forces.[2] But, in spite of these serious drawbacks, which tend to make education a mere mechanical process, Herbart's contributions to the science of pedagogy were most valuable and lasting.

Frœbel, the prince of modern educators, may be said to have been a pupil of Pestalozzi's. He, too, undertook to do what the latter had omitted, namely, to work out a system of pedagogical theory and practice, based upon the facts of human nature, and calculated to enable it to reach its fullest realization. Being an ardent student, and somewhat dreamy lover, of sub-human nature, he was, like Rousseau, prone to a kind of mystical nature-pantheism, which seriously interfered with the effect of his work, tending to render it sentimental, instead of rigorously scien-

[1] This comes out, with striking clearness, in his notion of requital, which he thinks is an ethical one. See De Garmo, *Herbart* (in this series), p. 52 ; cf. p. 56.

[2] Herbart's psychology has found many disciples, Lazarus, Steinthal, Fechner, Wundt, etc.; and a Frenchman, M. Fouillée, has written a book entitled *Les idées-forces*.

tific. This trait has communicated itself to many of his followers and done much mischief. In spite of this, Frœbel did more than any other man to work out a scheme for the gradual, orderly, and healthy development of the powers of the child, with a view to rendering him a social and moral being, a worthy member of the commonwealth of men and of the eternal kingdom of God. Like Herbart, Frœbel held that a moral life was the end of all education.

Alongside Pestalozzi, Herbart, and Frœbel, must be mentioned, among the disciples of Rousseau, a man far less known than they, but well deserving of careful study by all educators — Antonio Rosmini-Serbati (1797–1855).[1] This eminent thinker, one of the greatest of the century, derived his knowledge of Rousseau mainly through the writings of Madame Necker de Saussure, which he greatly admired. Protected by his Catholicism from pantheism, and entirely free from sentimentalism, Rosmini elaborated a scheme of education on the basis of his own philosophy. According to this, the human soul is a substantial feeling, rendered intelligent by having presented to it, as object, ideal, or universal and undetermined, being. This is at first the sole object and constituent of its consciousness. In the process of experience, the "fundamental feeling," which constitutes the subjective aspect of the soul, is modified and, at the same time, the indefinite object, being, is determined. In this way there gradually arises in the soul a world of

[1] See Father Lockhart's *Life*, and the briefer *Life* prefixed to my translation of Rosmini's *Philosophical System* (London, Kegan Paul).

feeling, referred to being, as substance and cause. In proportion as this being is defined through feeling, we see the truth, or God; for ideal being is but God undefined. Since all reality is feeling, and all ideality God unrealized, morality consists in so ordering our feelings that they shall gradually define God for us, and thus make us partakers in the Beatific Vision. However strange and mediæval this spiritual mysticism may seem, it enabled Rosmini to work out a scheme for the orderly development of a divine world in the consciousness of the child — a scheme which has very great value, even for those who cannot accept its presuppositions, being superior to those of Herbart and Frœbel in many important particulars. Unfortunately, it breaks off at the end of the fifth year of the child's life;[1] and we cannot but regret that a man so eminently fitted, by natural temperament, education, and psychological and philosophic insight, for pedagogical research, should not have been spared to complete his work.

To give an account of all the educators that have been influenced by the teaching of Rousseau would be to write the history of modern pedagogy. Enough has already been said to show the nature and extent of that influence, and to show how it has been modified and, in very large measure, counteracted.

As one reads *Émile*, he is sometimes tempted to believe that Rousseau wrote it merely to maintain a thesis which he did not believe, but wished to see dis-

[1] Besides the (incomplete) work above referred to (p. 110 n.), there is a volume of essays on *Pedagogics* by Rosmini, parts of which well deserve to be translated.

cussed, and threw it down, as a gauntlet, to challenge a world which had lost all real interest in education, and compel it to defend, if it could, its own practice. Whether so intended or not, this has certainly been the effect of the book. It has made men attempt to defend existing systems of education, and, finding that they could not, resolve and endeavor to discover better ones. And better ones have been discovered. We are gradually gaining light with regard to the nature and capacities of the child, and getting a clearer insight into the means by which they may be unfolded, and the destiny to which they tend. We now know that, instead of being an unreflective and immoral automaton up to the age of puberty,[1] he exercises intelligence and conscience — in rudimentary forms, indeed — from the hour of his birth. And so we conclude that he is to be governed from the first, not by the law of necessity, but by that of freedom and righteous love.

But, for all this, there is still much to be done in the sphere of education. We have, even now, no scientific theory of pedagogy, and the reason is that we have no scientific theory of human nature. We are still distracted and blinded to the truth, on the one hand, by certain traditional conceptions that once formed part of a view of the world-economy, long since rendered unbelievable and obsolete, and on the other by certain modern philosophic prejudices, of a dualistic sort, for which Kant is in the main responsible. The former make us still inclined to believe that the soul is a created substance, beyond the reach of experience, a transcendental monad possessed of certain fixed fac-

[1] Herbart wrote essays on the freedom of the will at fourteen.

ulties, and capable of being trained only in a certain definite direction to a fore-appointed end. The latter make us believe that it is a bundle of categories, empty thought-forms, existing prior to all sensation or experience, and conditioning it. In either case, we are irrationally induced to regard, and to talk about, the soul as something other than what by experience,[1] the only source of true knowledge, we know it to be, and thus to build our educational theories upon a mere chimera. There is not one fact in our experience going to show that the soul is either a substance or a bundle of categories. Indeed, when subtly considered, these words are absolutely without meaning. When we ask what we *know* the soul to be, we can only answer: A sentient desire, or desiderant feeling, which, through its own effort after satisfaction, gradually differentiates itself into a world, or, which is the same thing, gradually learns to refer its satisfactions to a world of things in time and space. Feeling is primary; ideas, or differentiations in feeling, are secondary — exactly the contrary of what Herbart believed. The world that we know, whether material or spiritual, is entirely made up of feeling differentiated by ideas. The end of education, therefore, can be none other than the complete satisfaction of feeling, by an ever-increasing harmonious, that is, unitary, differentiation of it into a world of sources of satisfaction. This satisfaction will be greater in proportion as the sources are more numerous and richer. Hence, every soul will be consulting

[1] This does not mean merely what is called "sense-experience," but includes all the intelligible phenomena of consciousness, even metaphysical ones.

for its own satisfaction, by doing its best to satisfy every other soul, and to make it as rich as possible. Thus the most perfect egoism will be found to be one with the most perfect altruism, and the law of virtue to be one with the law of blessedness, as, in the end it must be, unless all existence be a mockery. On this view of the soul, and on this alone, will it be possible to erect an intelligible and coherent structure of education, intellectual, affectional, and moral.

BRIEF BIBLIOGRAPHY

OF the numerous editions of the works of Rousseau the best is that by Musset-Pathay (Paris, Dupont, 1823), in twenty-three volumes octavo. A serviceable edition is that published by Hachette, Paris, 1865, in duodecimo.

The works of Rousseau which bear on the subject of education are these: —

1. *Has the Reëstablishment of the Sciences and Arts contributed to purify Morals?* with the *Letter to M. Grimm*, the *Reply to the King of Poland*, *Reply to M. Bordes*, and *Letter on a New Refutation* (published 1750 sq.).

2. *What is the Origin of Inequality among Men, and is it authorized by the Natural Law?* (1754).

3. *The New Héloïse* (1761).

4. *The Social Contract* (1762).

5. *Émile* (1762), with *Émile and Sophie, or the Solitaries* (written 1778).

6. *Letters to M. de Malesherbes* (1762).

7. *Letters from the Mountain* (1764).

8. *Political Economy* (in the *Encyclopédie*).

9. *Confessions* (written 1766-70; published, Part I., 1781; Part II., 1788).

10. *Rêveries* (written 1777-78).

The following are the best works on Rousseau: —

1. MUSSET-PATHAY, *Histoire de la Vie et des Ouvrages de J.-J. Rousseau*, Paris, 1821.

2. STRECKEISEN-MOULTOU, *Rousseau, ses Amis et ses Ennemis*, Paris, 1865.

3. H. BEAUDOIN, *La Vie et les Œuvres de J.-J. Rousseau*, Paris, 1871.

4. ST. MARC GIRARDIN, *J.-J. Rousseau, sa Vie et ses Œuvres*, Paris, 1875.

5. JOHN MORLEY, *Rousseau*, London and New York, 1891.

6. CHUQUET, *J.-J. Rousseau*, Paris, 1893.

There is interesting information regarding Rousseau and his influence to be found in Hermann Hettner's *Literaturgeschichte des XVIIIten Jahrhunderts*, Vol. II., pp. 431–517, and in H. Michel's *L'Idée de l'État*, pp. 37–45.

Of Rousseau's *Émile*, there exist several English translations, two of them made in the author's lifetime. The most accessible are these: —

Rousseau's Émile, or Treatise on Education. Abridged and annotated by William H. Payne, Ph.D., LL.D. New York: D. Appleton & Co., 1893.

Rousseau's Émile, or Concerning Education. Extracts with an Introduction and Notes, by Jules Steeg. Boston: D. C. Heath & Co., 1885.

INDEX

A

Abélard, 5 *note* 2.
Academies, 149, 176.
Adolescence, 156 *sqq*.
Æschylus, 6 *note* 2.
Æsthetic theory, 175.
Agnosticism, 167 *note* 1, 225 *note* 2.
Agriculture, 144.
Agrippa, Menenius, 11 *note* 4.
Al Ghazzali, 203.
Alembert. See D'Alembert.
Althusen, 20.
Altruism, 244.
American boy, 123.
Animal food, 132 *sq*.
Annecy, 36, 41.
Anthropomorphism, 165.
Antigone, 128 *note*.
Antony, Mark, 25 *note*.
Aquinas, Thomas, 203.
Archimandrite, 42.
Aristotle, 77, 89, 97, 223.
Aristotle (Davidson), 79, 101 *note* 1, 141 *notes*.
Armenian costume, 66.
Astronomy, 189 *sqq*.
Automaton, 128.

B

Báb, the, 91.
Bacon, Francis, 8.
Balfour, Arthur, 225 *note*.
Bellamy, Edward, 93.
Bellegarde, Mdlle. de, 55.
Berlin, 67.
Berne, 66.
Bienne, Lake of, 66.
Blacksmithing, 141.
Bodin, 20.

Books, 133, 135, 142.
Bossey, 29 *sqq*.
Bossuet, *Hist. Univ.*, 27.
Bourgoin, 69.
Bowen, H. C. (*Frœbel*), 219.
Boyhood, 187 *sqq*.
Broglie, Mde. de, 52.
Browning, Mrs., 6 *note* 1.
Bryce, James, 4 *note* 1.
Buddhist, 169.
Burns, Robert, 145 *note* 2, 230.
Burton (*Hume*), 159 *note*.

C

Cæsar, Julius, 25 *note*, 161 *note*.
Cakes and candy, 129 *note* 2.
Calais, 69.
Calvinism, 15.
Candy, 129 *note* 2, 131.
Carlyle, Thomas, 231 *note*.
Carpenter, Edward, 120 *note*.
Carpentry, 144.
Catechumens, Hospice of, 36.
Categorical imperative, 194, 195 *note*, 223.
Cecil (*Pseudo-Philosophy*), 225 *note* 2.
Chambéry, 44 *sqq*., 69.
Character of Rousseau, 31, 71 *sqq*.
Charles II., 15.
Charmettes, Les, 45, 66, 187 *note*.
Childhood, 113 *sqq*.
Children, Rousseau's, 55, 105 *note*.
Chivalry, 217.
Cities, 196, 210.
Clarke, Samuel, 166 *sq*.
Comenius, 236.
Common sense, 133.
Commonwealth, 12.

Condillac, Abbé, 47, 55.
Confession of Faith. See Savoyard Vicar.
Confessions (Rousseau's), 3, 35, 38, 41, 45, 50, 67, 68, 79, 105 *note*, 128 *note* 1, 158 *note* 2, 177.
Confignon, 36.
Conti, Prince de, 65, 69.
Contract, social, 10 *sqq.*, 16 *sqq.*
Corsica, 67.
Country, 196.
Criticism, Kantian, 167 *note* 1, 224.
Critique of the Pure Reason, 224.
Critique of Judgment, 225.
Culture, 80, 98, 100, 102, 175, 218, 223, 234.
Curiosity, 189.
Cyclopean freedom, 218.

D

D'Alembert, 56, 63, 68.
Dalliers, 24.
Dante, 3, 4 *notes*, 11 *note* 2, 101 *note*, etc.
Darwin, Charles, 129 *note* 2.
Davenport (Mr)., 68.
Death of Rousseau, 70.
Declaration of Independence, 233.
De Garmo, Charles (*Herbart*), 239 *note*.
Denzinger (*Enchiridion*), 5 *note* 1.
Derbyshire, 68.
Descartes, 8, 45, 92 *note*, 164 *note*, 168.
Devin du Village, 59.
Dialogues (Rousseau's), 70.
Diderot, 51, 55 *sqq.*, 63.
Dijon, Academy of, 56, 81.
Discourse on *Progress of Arts*, 56, 77.
Discourse on *Inequality*, 66, 77, 83 *sqq.*
Doctor, 180 *note* 3.
Dogma, 164, 182 *sqq.*
Domain, public, 255.
Dover, 69.
Dress, change of, 59.
Drummond, Henry, 255.
Duclos, 174.

E

Economics, 234.
Eden, 80.
Education by nature, 102, 210, 236 *sqq.*
Egoism, 244.
Eliot, George, 169 *note* 1.
Emerson, R. W., 151 *note* 1, 156, 210 *note*, 231.
Émile, 62 *sqq.*, 70, 77, 97 *sqq.*
Émile's travels, 195.
Encyclopaedists, 63.
Encyclopédie, 56.
England, 67.
English, the, 133.
Epicureanism, 190, 215, 234 *sq.*
Épinay, Mde. d', 55, 61, 62.
Equality, 9, 16.
Ermenonville, 70 *sq.*
Ethical system, Rousseau's, 234.
Europeans, 196.
Existence, social and moral, 214.

F

Fastidiousness, 109.
Faust. See Gœthe.
Fechner, 231 *note*.
Feeling, 85 *note*, 91, 108 *note*, 158, 213, 243.
Filmer, Sir Robert, 16.
Fontenelle, 28, 51.
Form, sense of, 132.
Fouillée, 239 *note* 2.
Frederick the Great, 65 *sq.*, 68.
Freedom, 11, 18, 198, 220.
French language, 176.
Frœbel, 238 *sqq.*

G

Gaime, Abbé, 38.
Gâtier, M., 40 and *note.*
Gaures, the, 133.
Generosity, 126.
Geneva, and Lake, 26, 41, 60, 65.
Gentlemanliness, 81, 217.
Geography, 130.
Girls' education, 178 *sqq.*
Girardin, M., 70.
Gluttony, 182.

INDEX

Gœthe (*Faust*), 5 *note* 3, 7 *note* 2, 24, 25 *note*, 50 *note*, 104 *note* 1, 113, 117 *note* 1, 225 *note* 3, 229 ; (*Wilh. Meister*), 225 *note* 3, 229.
"Good Time," 120.
Gouvon, Comte de, 38.
Grammar, 133.
Greek, 176.
Grenoble, 69.
Gretchen (*Faust*), 50 *note*.
Grimm, 63, 129 *note* 2.
Grotius, Hugo, 20, 196 *sq*.

H

Habit, 108.
Hamlet, 25 *note*.
Handicraft, 145 and *note* 2.
Hatch (*Hibbert Lect.*), 7 *note* 1.
Hearing, 132.
Hegel, 14 *note* 4, 211, 226.
Helvétius, 169.
Herbart, 238, 242 *sq*.
Herbart, De Garmo, 239 *note* 1.
Hermes of Praxiteles, 216 *sq*.
Hermitage, the, 60, 66.
Herodotus, 161 *note*.
Hiero's fountain, 39.
History, 133, 153, 161 *sq*.
Hobbes (*Leviathan*), 8 *sqq*., 77, 80, 97, 100, 196 *sq*.
Homer, 189, 218 *note*.
Hooker, 14 *note* 3, 20, 77.
Houdetot, Comtesse d', 55, 61.
Humanists, 6.
Hume, David, 67, 80 *note*, 103 *note*, 159 *note*, 224.
Hurons, 149.
Huxley, 92 *note*, 167 *note* 1, 222 *note*.

I

Ideas, 85, 138, 152, 243.
Independence, Declaration of, 86, 233.
Individualism, 4.
Industry, 146.
Infancy, 97 *sqq*.
Inheritance, 147.
Intolerance, 184, 215.
Islâm, 15.
Italian language, 176.

J

Jacobite, 65.
James, William, 228, 225 *note* 2.
James II., 16.
Jerusalem, 42.
Jesuits, 51, 98, 129 *note* 2.
Jordan, Wilhelm, 203.
Judgment, evil of, 150, 152.
Jura, Mt., 66.
Jus Naturale, 124.
Justice, 124.
Justinian (*Institutes*), 11 *note* 3, 14 *note* 2.

K

Kant, 86 *note*, 103 *note*, 195 *note*, 224 *sq*., 242.
Keats, John, 230 *note* 1.
Keith, Marshal, 65 *sq*., 67.
Kidd, Benjamin, 225 *note*.
King Lear, 85, 100 *note* 1.
Kleist, Fr. von, 210.
Kœrner, Theodor, 229.

L

Labor, division of, 84 ; duty of, 145 *sq*.
La Bruyère, 28.
La Fontaine, 133.
Lambercier, M. and Mdlle., 29 *sqq*.
Language, 85, 133.
Latin, 29, 38, 40, 175.
Lausanne, 41.
Law of Nature, 9 *sqq*., 21 *sqq*.
Lazarus, 239 *note* 2.
Learning, despised by Rousseau, 149.
Leibniz, 45.
Lersch (*Sprachphilosophie*), 6 *note* 2.
Le Sueur (*Hist. of Church*, etc.), 27.
Levite of Ephraim, 65.
Lex Naturalis, 9.
Liberty, 9, 11, 118.
Life, 147.
Lincolnshire, 69.
Literature, 133.
Livy, 11 *note* 4, 161 *note*.
Locke, John, 8, 16 *sqq*., 45, 78 *note*, 80, 97, 98, 163, 236.
London, 67.

INDEX

Lowell, J. R., 99 *note* 2, 128 *note*.
Luxembourg, Duke and Duchess of, 62 *sqq*., 105 *note*.
Lying, 126.
Lyons, 40, 43, 47, 51.

M

Mably, M. de, 47.
Macbeth, 220 *note*.
Machiavelli, 20.
Magician, 140 *sq*.
Magnetism, 140 *sq*.
Maine, Sir H. S., 92 *note* 3.
Malebranche, 8, 45.
Malesherbes, M. de, 74, 77.
"Mamma," 41 and often.
Manhood, 208 *sqq*.
Manual training, 145.
Marriage of Rousseau, 69.
Marriage of Émile, 201.
Marseilles, 204.
Marsiglio di Padova, 20.
Meaning, 228.
Mecca, Meccans, 97, 165.
Mercure de France, 56.
Metaphysics, 153.
Mirabeau, Marquis de, 69.
Molière, 28.
Monquin, 69.
Montaigu, Comte de, 52 *sq*.
Montesquieu, 20 *sq*., 197.
Montmorency, 62 *sq*.
Montpellier, 46.
Moors, 207.
Morals, 153.
Morelly, 20 *sq*.
Morley, J. (*Rousseau*), 4, 80 *note*.
Motiers, 66.
Muhammad, 91, 99.

N

Nairne, Lady, 230.
Nani (*Hist. of Venice*), 28.
Naples, 204.
Narcisse, 51, 59.
Natural rights, 89.
Nature, 6, 8 *sqq*., 22, 80, 83, 97, 100 *sq*., 102, 107, 117, 120 *sq*., 175, 187, 218, 222 *note*, 223, 229 *sq*., 234; law of, 9 *sqq*.; state of, 8 *sqq*.
Necessity, 120.
Necker de Saussure, Mde., 240.
Neo-Catholics, 227.
Neuchâtel, 41, 65.
New Héloïse, 62 *sq*., 210, 215, 224 *note*.
Noblesse oblige, 119.
Notation, musical, 51.
Nyon, 32, 41.

O

Obscurantism, 150, 225.
Oversoul, 231.
Ovid (*Metamorphoses*), 28.
Oyster's universe, 97, 131.

P

Pantheon, 71.
Paris, 42, 47 *sqq*., 69 *sqq*., 175, 177.
Pascal, Blaise, 8.
Passions, 159.
Patriarcha, 16.
Pays de Vaud, 32.
Pension offered to Rousseau, 67.
Perception, 152.
Persifleur, Le, 55.
Persona, 11 *note* 3.
Pestalozzi, 237 *sq*.
Peter the Great, 93.
Philopistism, 225 and *note* 2.
Philosophy of Rousseau, 85, 224.
Plato, 6 and *note* 2, 7, 93, 187, 162 *note*.
Plutarch (*Lives*), 27.
Politeness, 174.
Political Economy, 234.
Political right, 196 *sq*.
Pontverre, M. de, 36.
Poor, education of the, 106 *note*.
Poplars, Isle of, 70.
Port Royal *Logic*, 45.
Postulates of Pure Reason, 106, 224.
Praxiteles, 216 *sq*.
Princes, 16.
Problem of society, 86.
Property, private, 234 *sq*.
Protestantism, 227.

Q

Quintilian, 141 *note* 1.

R

Reading, 134.
Reason, 6, 8, 22 *sq.*, 138.
Recreation, 151.
Reflection, 151.
Reformation, its claims, 5, 7.
Reformers, 6.
Religion, 168, 165, 182 *sqq.*, 227.
Renaissance, its claims, 5 *sq.*
Revelation, 8 *sq.*, 22 *sq.*, 86, 98.
Rêveries, 70.
Revolution, American, 238.
Riding, 130.
Ritschl, 227.
Robbers (Schiller's), 229.
Robespierre, 227.
Robinson Crusoe, 148 *sqq.*, 154, 210.
Romanticism, 224.
Rome, 165.
Romola (George Eliot's), 104 *note* 2.
Rosmini, 119 *note*, 240 *sqq.* and *notes*.
Rousseau, Jean-Jacques, character and importance, 8, 27; individualism, 4; outcome of Renaissance, 5; follows Hobbes, 8; literary style, 25; birth, parentage, and education, 26 *sqq.*; his brother, 26 *note*; temperament, 28; at Bossey, 29; sensuality, 31; return to, and life at, Geneva, 31; apprenticeship, 32 *sq.*; a tramp, 33 *sqq.*; his master's character, 34; becomes a Catholic and goes to Mde. de Warens, 36; crosses the Alps to Turin, 36; life there, 37 *sq.*; theft, cruelty, lying, and indecency, 38; tramps back to Chambéry, 39; deserts musician in Lyons, 39 *sq.*; is deserted by Mde. de Warens, 41; meets his father at Nyon and goes to Freiburg, 41; turns music-teacher at Lausanne and Neuchâtel, 41; follows Greek archimandrite, but is rescued from him at Soleure, 42; goes on foot to Paris, 42; leaves it and goes south, learning on the way the condition of the people, 42 *sq.*; returns to Mde. de Warens, 43; relations with her, 44; becomes surveyor's clerk, 44; throws up employment, 44; tries again to teach music, 44; new relations with Mde. de Warens, 45; reads Latin, geometry, philosophy, etc., 45; suffers from languors, vapors, and fear of hell, 45; becomes an invalid, and goes to Montpellier; vulgar intrigue on the way, 46; "virtuously" returns to Mde. de Warens, to find his place taken; first sense of duty, 46; leaves Chambéry for Paris, 47; review of early life and character, 48; reception in Paris; ill success of musical project; meets Fontenelle and Diderot, 51; secretary of embassy in Venice; experiences there, 52; returns to Paris, and lodges near the Luxembourg; meets Thérèse Le Vasseur (1744), 53; life with her, 54; spends autumn of 1747 at Chenonceau; child born and exposed; fate of other children, 55; has a revelation due to Dijon Academy's prize-offer, 56 *sq.*; wins the prize, 58; performance of his operas, 59; second discourse, on Inequality, 60; visits Geneva with Thérèse and returns to Protestantism, 60; goes to the Hermitage at Montmorency, and gives himself up to dreaming and his passion for Mde. d'Houdetot, 61; quarrels with Mde. d'Épinay and moves to village of Montmorency; writes *New Héloïse*, *Social Contract*, and *Émile*, 62 *sq.*; becomes acquainted with Duke and Duchess of Luxembourg; *Émile* condemned, 63 *sq.*; persecution and flight; *Levite of Ephraim*, 65; stops at Yverdun, 65; settles at Motiers, and is befriended by Marshal Keith, 66; driven thence, settles on Isle of St.

Peter, 66; driven thence, goes, *via* Paris, with Hume to England, 67; success in London, 67; settles at Wootton, 68; quarrels with Hume, 68 *sq.*; returns to France, 69; moves about to Trye (near Gisors), Grenoble, Bourgoin (where he informally marries Thérèse), Monquin, 69; returns to Paris and lives there for eight years; his *Dialogues*, *Rêveries*, etc., written; goes to Ermenonville, dies and is buried, 70; ashes removed to Pantheon, 71; his character, 71-76; inventor of manual training, 145; his ideal of life, 177 *sq.*; his ethics, 184 *note* 2, 185; his influence, 211 *sqq.*; defects of his system, 211 *sqq.*; effect on religion, 227; father of democracy, 232.

Ruskin, 231 *note*.
Russia and Russians, 93 *note*.

S

St. Andiol, 46.
St. Esprit, 46.
St. Just, 227.
St. Peter, Isle of, 66.
Savage life, 99.
Savoy, 36.
Savoyard Vicar, 38, 40, 64, 165 *sqq.*, 224 *note* 2, 226.
Scævola, Mucius, 28.
Schiller, 211, 229.
Schopenhauer, 208 *note*.
Science, 133.
Scythians, 196.
Sensations, 152.
Sepulchre, Holy, 42.
Sexuality, 157, 217.
Shakespeare, 9 *note*, 100 *note* 1, 220 *note*.
Slavery, 209, 220.
Small-pox, 130.
Smell, sense of, 132.
Smith, Joseph, 91.
Social Contract, 62, 77, 78 *sqq.*, 197, 198 *note*.

Socialism, 4, 234 *sqq.*
Social Sympathies, 160 *sqq.*
Society, 161.
Socrates, 7, 79.
Soleure, 42.
Solitaries, The, 203 *sqq.*
Sophie, 185 *sqq.*, 203 *sqq.*
Sophists, 79.
Sophocles, 128 *note*.
Soul, nature of, 243.
Sovereign, 11 *sq.*, 87 *sqq.*
Space, 132,
Spectator, The, 192.
Spencer, Herbert, 125 *note* 3.
Spinoza, 145 *note* 1, 164 *note*.
Steinthal, 239 *note* 2.
Stoicism, 190, 199, 215, 218, 232, 234 *sq.*
Subjectivism, 1.
Swimming, 130.

T

Tacitus, 161 *note*.
Taste, 175.
Taxation, 235.
Télémaque, 186, 192.
Tennyson, 25 *note*, 77, 92 *note*, 144 *note*, 156, 208, 211, 224 *note* 2.
Thérèse Le Vasseur, 53 *sqq.*, 58 *sqq.*, 68 *sq.*
Thoreau, H. D., 144 *note*.
Thucydides, 161 *note*.
Travelling, 195 *sqq.*
Trent, Council of, 4.
Turin, 36 *sq.*

U

Unitarianism, 227.
Unsocial education, 218.
Usefulness, 141 *sq.*
Utopia, 93.

V

Vaccination, 130.
Vanity, 141 *note* 1.
Venice, 52.
Vercellis, Mde. de, 37 *sq.*
Vincennes, 56 *sq.*
Voltaire, 5, 25, 60, 68 *sq.*, 67, 68, 83, 226, 227, 229.

W

Walden (Thoreau's), 144 *note*.
Walpole, Horace, 68 *note*.
Warens, Mde. de, 36, 39 *sqq*., 43 *sqq*., 187 *note*.
Werther, Sorrows of, 229.
Wilhelm Meister, 25 *note*.
Will, general, 90.
Willers, 24.
Women, 178 *sqq*., 217.
Wootton, 68 *sq*.
Wordsworth, 99, 151 *note* 1, 230 *note* 2.

Work, duty of, 145 *sq*.
Writing, 135.
Wundt, Wilh., 239 *note* 2.

X

Xenophon, 161 *note*.

Y

Youth, 178 *sqq*.
Yverdun, 65.

Z

Zamori (von Kleist's), 210.